AN INTRODUCTION TO
PORIFERA

AN INTRODUCTION TO PORIFERA

By
H.S. Bhamrah
Kavita Juneja

Edited by
Balvinder K.

ANMOL PUBLICATIONS PVT. LTD.
NEW DELHI - 110 002 (INDIA)

ANMOL PUBLICATIONS PVT. LTD.
4374/4B, Ansari Road, Daryaganj
New Delhi - 110 002

An Introduction to Porifera

First Edition, 1991
Reprint, 1992, 1999
Second Revised Edition, 2001

ISBN 81-261-0675-1

PRINTED IN INDIA

Published by J.L. Kumar for Anmol Publications Pvt. Ltd., New Delhi - 110 002 and Printed at Mehra Offset Press, Delhi.

Contents

PREFACE

An Introduction to Porifera is the revised and enlarged second edition of the book. It has been designed to approach the morphology, anatomy, physiology and development of selected type in a simple and lucid style. The approach to the discussion of all the types is very simple so as to impact to the students a clear and vivid understanding. According to the scheme of treatment the important animal types of the phylum have been dealt with first, and efforts have been made to present their elaborate and uptodate account. General characters and classification and brief description of other important types of the phylum have also been dealt with complete, authentic and uptodate account. Further separate chapters on topics of significance and general interest pertaining to the phylum have also been added to make the treatment more elaborate.

It has been the constant endeavour of the authors to furnish maximum substance, keeping in view the limitations of size of the volume. Efforts have been made to condense the matter as far as practicable. The book features both a text and a laboratory guide. It is hoped that this book will not only meet the requirement of Indian students but will also be useful as a guideline to the teachers in their teaching.

There can be no claim to originality except in the manner of treatment and much of the information has been obtained from the books and scientific journals available in different libraries.

The authors express their thanks to their friends and colleagues whose constant inspiration have initiated them to bring out this book.

In this edition all the errors of first edition have been rectified. New information is incorporated in the light of recent developments and latest research. Teachers and scholars can send their criticism and suggestions to further improve the contents.

Authors

1

Porifera : Characters & Classification

Sponges which constitute phylum Porifera, are the most primitive of the multicellular animals. Neither true tissues nor organs are present, and the cells display a considerable degree of independence. All the members of the phylum are sessile and exhibit little detectable movement. This combination of characteristic convinced *Aristotle, Pliny,* and other ancient naturalists that sponges were plants. In fact it was not until 1765, when internal water current was first observed by *Ellis*, that the animal nature of sponges became clearly established. As a result, *Linnaeus, Lamarck* and *Cuvier* placed the sponges under Zoophytes or Polypes in their systems, regarding them as allied to anthozoan coelenterates, and many investigators sought to find in sponges the polyps they thought must be there. *de Blaiville* (1816) recognized the lack of affinities of sponges with coelenterates and separated them into a group Spongiaria allied to Protozoa, but this idea gained little attention, and, through much of the 19th century, sponges were placed with coelenterates, usually under the name Coelenterata or Coelentera or Radiata. Morphology and Physiology of sponges were first understood by *Robert E.Grant* (1825), who coined the term Porifera (L. *Porous* = pore; *ferro* = to bear). *Huxley* (1875) and *Sollas* (1884) proposed the complete separation of Sponges from other Metazoa on the ground of many peculiarities, but this view did not find its present general acceptance until about the beginning of 20th century. Sponges are now recognized as constituting a separated isolated branch of the Metazoa, named Parazoa, after *Sollas*.

General Characters

1. All sponges are aquatic, mostly marine but a few are fresh-water.
2. They are multicellular organisms with *cellular grade of body organization* without forming tissues or organs.
3. They are sessile, solitary or colonial.
4. They have asymmetrical or radially symmetrical bodies.

5. The body is cylindrical, tubular or vase-like.
6. The body wall is diploblastic with outer dermal epithelium and inner gastral epithelium with a gelatinous non-cellular mesenchyme in between.
7. The body surface bears numerous minute pores i.e. ostia for the ingression of water.
8. They possess peculiar canal system through which water current flows drawing food and oxygen inside the body and carrying away excretory and reproductive products.
9. Internal skeleton is present in the mesenchyme in the form of calcareous or siliceous spicules or of proteinous spongin fibres.
10. Digestion is entirely intracellular.
11. Nervous and sensory cells are lacking.
12. All sponges possess great power of regeneration.
13. They are mostly bisexual but asexual forms also exist.
14. Reproduction takes place both by asexual and sexual methods.
15. Asexual reproduction takes place by *budding, fission* or *gemmule* formation and sexual reproduction by sperms and ova.
16. Fertilization is internal and at the same time it is cross fertilization.
17. Cleavage is holoblastic and development is indirect followed by a free swimming ciliated larva, the *amphiblastula* or *parenchymula*.

CLASSIFICATION

The classification of sponges presented great difficulty, and no one scheme has been unanimously accepted by specialists on sponges. The classification is based on the type of skeleton, and this serves to mark off rather sharply two groups of sponges, the calcareous and the glass sponges. The remaining silicons and horny sponges are, however, less clearly delimited, and they are variously subdivided by different workers. The classification here adopted is that given by *Topsent, Wilson* and *de Laubenfels*.

Phylum Porifera is divided into three classes:

Class-1. Calcarea

The members of this class possess their skeleton composed of separate calcareous spicules made of calcium carbonate (L.; *Caleis*= lime; Gr; *sponges* = sponge).

1. Members of this class are smaller in size, extending upto 15 cm. in length; may be solitary or colonial. All are marine.
2. Shape of body usually cylindrical or vase-like.

3. Osculum is narrow, terminal and fringed with spicules.
4. The colour of the body is white or dull-brown.
5. Skeleton consists of spicules which may be monaxon, triradiate or tetraradiate.
6. Collar cells or choanocytes are comparatively large.
7. The canal system is ascon, sycon or leucon type.

Order (i)-Homocoela

1. Body is small, cylindrical and thin walled without any foldings.
2. Canal system ascon type.
3. Spongocoel is lined throughout by choanocytes.

   Examples: *Leucosolenia, Clathrina*.

Order (ii)-Heterocoela

1. Body is comparatively bigger, vase-like, thick walled with internal foldings.
2. Canal system sycon or leucon type.
3. Choanocytes are restricted to the flagellated chambers.
4. Spongocoel is lined by dermal epithelium.

   Examples: *Scypha* or *Sycon, Grantia*.

Class 2. Hexactinellida or Triaxonida

The members of the class are called *glass-sponges* having triaxon or hexactinal spicules made up of silica.

1. Members of this class are of moderate size, extending up to one meter in length and are usually solitary.
2. The body shape is usually cylindrical, cup-shaped or funnel-shaped.
3. The osculum is wide and usually covered over by a siliceous sieve plate.
4. The skeleton consists of triaxon or hexactinal siliceous spicules, often fused resembling spun glass.
5. Dermal epithelium is wanting.
6. The canal system is simple rhagon type.
7. The choanocyte cells are restricted to finger-like flagellated chambers.
8. They are exclusively marine and occur chiefly in tropical deep sea water.

   Class Hexactinellida is divided into two orders :

Order (i)-Hexasterophora

1. The beautiful glass-like body is cylindrical, very light and attached to

the substratum directly.

2. The spicules are hexasters having star-like appearance.
3. The flagellated chambers are radially and regularly arranged.

Example: *Euplectella* (Venus's flower basket).

Order (ii)-Amphidiscophora

1. The body is usually rounded or oval and attached to the substratum by root tufts.
2. The spicules are amphidiscs having a convex disc, bearing a crown of backwardly directed marginal teeth at both ends.
3. The flagellated chambers are irregularly arranged.

Example: *Hyalonema* (Glass rope sponge).

Class 3. Demospongiae

This class comprises diverse and complicated sponges with skeleton of siliceous spicules or spongin fibres or a combination of both or totally absent. (Gr., *demos* = frame; *spongos* = sponge).

1. Members of this class are highly organised, varying from small to large size and may be solitary or colonial.
2. The body shape is variable being rounded, oval, cup-like or funnel-like.
3. The skeleton is made up of silicious spicules or spongin fibres or both. The spicules are monaxon or tetraxon.
4. Canal system is complicated and leucon type.
5. Choanocytes are restricted to small flagellated chambers.
6. They are mostly marine but few sponges are fresh water.

Class Demospongiae is divided into three sub-classes:

Subclass-I. Tetractinellida

1. Body is rounded or flattened.
2. Siliceous spicules, if present are tetraxon, or absent.
3. Spongin fibres are absent.

Order (i) Myxospongida

1. Spicules are absent.
2. Body surface is velvet-like

Example: *Oscarella*.

Order (ii) Carnosa

1. Homogenous leuconoid structure.
2. Spicules are of equal-size.

Examples: *Chondrilla, Plankina, Halina.*

Order (iii) Choristidia

1. Body form is usually elaborate:
2. Both small (microscleres) and large (megascleres) spicules are present.

Example: *Geodia, Ancoria.*

Subclass-II. Monaxonida

1. Body form variable, occurring in shallow and deep water.
2. The skeleton consists of monaxon spicules distinguished into megascleres only.
3. Spongin fibres may or may not be present.

Sub-class Monaxonida is divided into four orders:

Order (i) Hadromerina

(i) Megascleres are mostly tylostyles i.e. the broad end is knobbed.
(ii) Microscleres are usually absent and if present, are star-like.
(iii) Spongin fibres are absent.

Examples: *Cliona* (Boring sponge), *Suberites, Poterion.*

Order (ii) Halichondrina

(i) Megascleres are always of more than one kind.
(ii) Microscleres are usually absent.
(iii) Spongin fibres are present but they are very scanty.

Example: *Halichondria.*

Order (iii) Poecilosclerina

1. Megascleres are usually of two or more kinds and united by spongin fibres into a regular network.
2. Microscleres may be curved, bow-shaped or C-shaped.

Examples: *Myxilla, Microciona.*

Order (iv) Haplosclerina

(i) Megascleres are always diactinal and pointed at both ends.
(ii) Microscleres may or may not be present.
(iii) Spongin fibres are usually present.

Examples: *Chalina, Spongilla* (fresh-water), *Haliclona.*

Subclass-III. Keratosa

(i) The body form is usually rounded and massive with a leathery surface and dark colour, occurring generally in warm shallow water.
(ii) The skeleton is exclusively composed of spongin fibres.

(iii) The spicules are totally absent.

Examples: *Euspongia* (Bath sponge), *Hippospongia* (Horse sponge).

CLATHRINA

Phylum	-	Porifera
Class	-	Calcarea.
Order	-	Homocoela
Genus	-	*Clathrina*

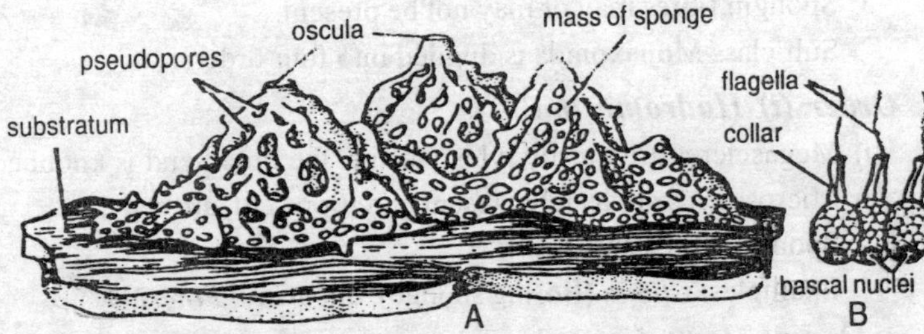

Fig. 1.1. *Clathrina*. A—Colony of *Clathrina clathrus;* B—Choanocytes of *Clathrina coriaca*.

1. It is a simple, marine sponge attached to the hard substratum.
2. It is sedentary sponge with a free end containing *osculum*.
3. The surface is perforated by minute apertures called *ostia*, through which the water enters the body. Canal system *asconoid type*.
4. Skeleton consists of calcareous spicules which are triradiate with equal rays.
5. Choanocytes lines the spongocoel.
6. Dermal membrane or cortex is lacking.
7. Development includes a *parenchymula* larva and the so called *olynthus stage*.

GRANTIA

Phylum	-	Porifera
Class	-	Calcarea
Order	-	Heterocoela
Genus	-	*Grantia*

1. It is a small, solitary or colonial, marine sponge.

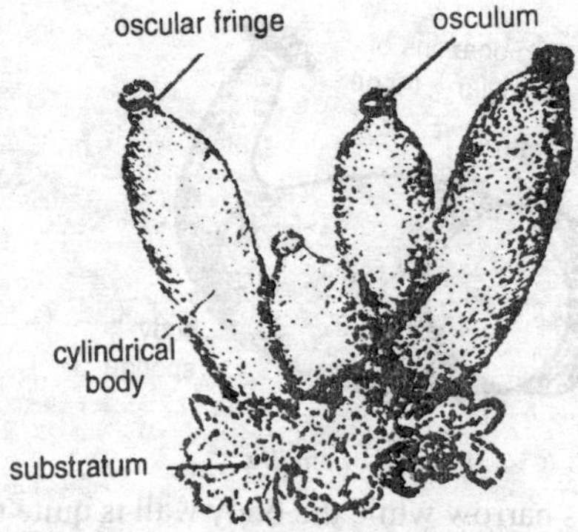

Fig. 1.2. *Grantia.*

2. It is found in the Gulf of St. Lawrence.
3. The body is complex vase-like.
4. Each cylinder bulges in the centre and opens to the exterior by an osculum.
5. The osculum is encircled by a fringe of large giant monaxon spicules forming oscular fringe.
6. The body surface is covered by the dermal membrane forming a cortex of varying thickness having special cortical spicules. The spicules are tangentially radiate.
7. Body wall is composed of outer dermal epidermis, middle mesenchyme and inner flattened epithelium lining the spongocoel.
8. Canal system is syconoid.
9. Choanocytes are restricted to the radial canal, and the flagella arise directly from nuclei.
10. Bisexual. Reproduction by asexual and sexual methods. Asexual reproduction by budding and regeneration. Sexual by gametes. Larva is an *amphiblastula*.

LEUCILLA

The classification is the same as that of *Grantia.*

1. It is a small, marine and solitary sponge.
2. It is found in Europe and U.S.A.
3. The body is somewhat globose in shape as the anterior region is narrow and the posterior region is broad.
4. The osculum is situated at the anterior most end and is surrounded by oscular fringe of monaxon spicules.

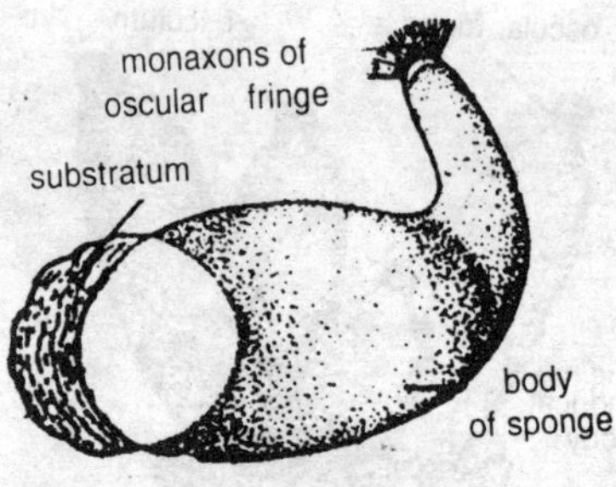

Fig. 1.3. *Leucilla.*

5. The spongocoel is narrow while the body wall is quite thick.
6. Canal system is primitive leuconoid type. Each radial canal is subdivided into elongated flagellated chambers grouped around a common excurrent canal.
7. The skeleton is of inarticulate type.

LEUCANDRA

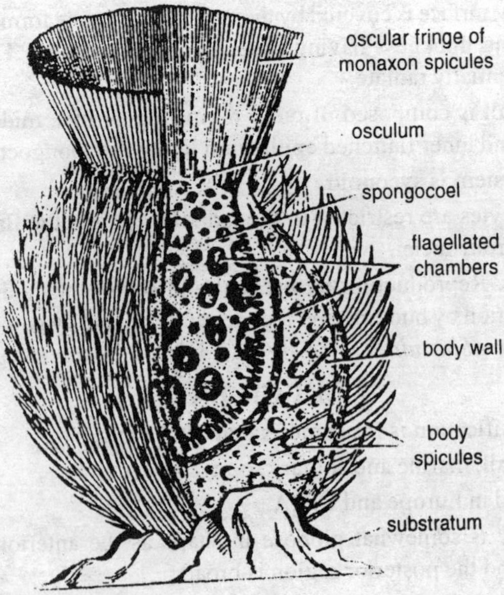

Fig. 1.4. *Leucandra.*

The systematic position is the same as that of *Grantia.*

1. It is a small, marine and solitary sponge.
2. Body is globose in shape.
3. Body wall is thick. Osculum is situated at the anterior end and is surrounded by oscular fringe of monaxon spicules.
4. Dermal skeleton is formed of tangentially arranged triradiate spicules which may sometimes develop an apical ray.
5. The flagellated chambers are small and spheroidal.

OSCARELLA

Phylum	-	Porifera
Class	-	Demospongiae
Subclass	-	Tetractinellida
Order	-	Maxospongida
Genus	-	*Oscarella*

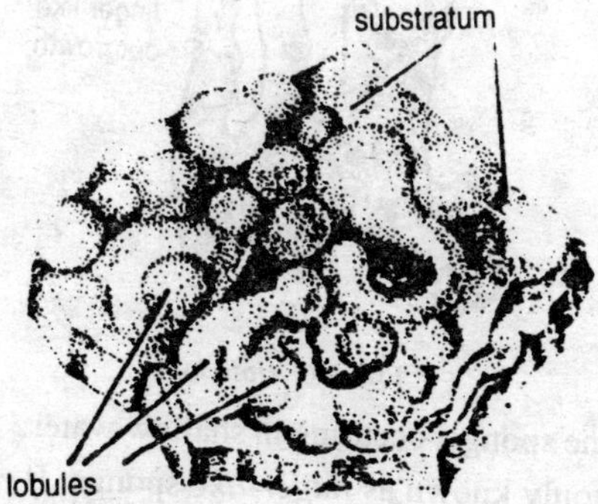

Fig. 1.5. *Oscarella.*

1. It is found in shallow water forming encrustation over the rocks and submerged objects.
2. It occurs in British water.
3. It is a bright coloured small sponge whose upper surface is lobulated.
4. The canal system is *leuconoid type*.
5. The lobules are covered with thin dermal layer. Each lobule contains excurrent canal surrounded by flagellated chambers and the depression between the lobules house the incurrent canal.
6. Skeleton is absent i.e. the spicules are completely absent.

HALICLONA

Phylum	-	Porifera
Class	-	Demospongiae
Subclass	-	Monaxonida
Order	-	Haplosclerina
Genus	-	*Haliclona*

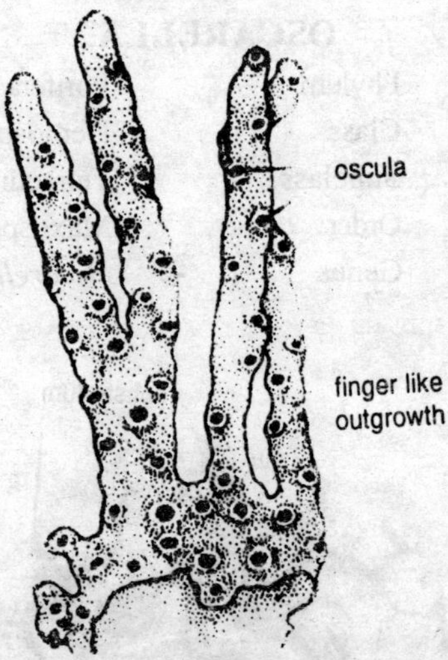

Fig. 1.6. *Haliclona.*

1. It is a marine sponge, occuring in shallow water.
2. It is commonly known as *finger-like* sponge. It remains attached to hard objects.
3. Body consists of several finger-like projections.
4. Each projection bears several oscula.
5. The canal system is *leuconoid type*.
6. The spicules are of various types.
7. Reproduction asexually by budding.

CHONDRILLA

Phylum	-	Porifera
Class	-	Demospongiae
Subclass	-	Tetractinellida

Order	-	Carnosa
Genus	-	*Chondrilla*

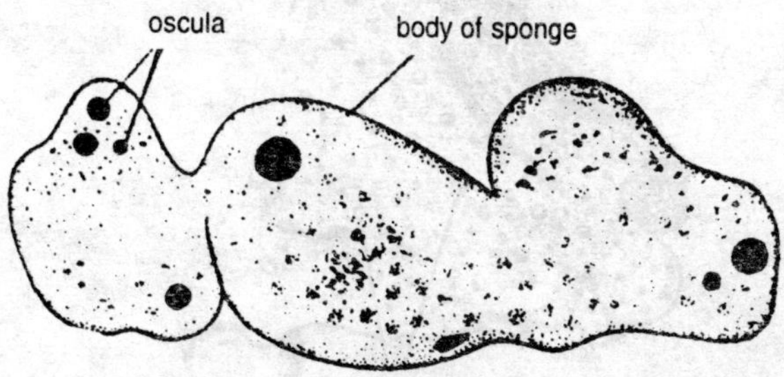

Fig. 1.7. *Chondrilla.*

1. It is a marine sponge found in British water and U.S.A.
2. The entire body looks like a rounded mass hence commonly called *chicken-liver* sponge.
3. The body remains attached to rocks etc.
4. Free surface contains few oscula.
5. Body surface is smooth, but mesogloea is thick and stony due to spherasters.
6. The spherasters found in cortex between the cones and are well developed while other spicules are absent.
7. Canal system is *leuconoid type*.

CLIONA

Phylum	-	Porifera
Class	-	Demospongiae
Subclass	-	Monaxonida
Order	-	Hadromerina
Genus	-	*Cliona*

1. It forms low encrustation on rocks, mollusc shells, coral skeleton and other calcareous objects.
2. It is cosmopolitan in distribution.
3. It is commonly called *Boring sponge* or *Sulphur sponge*.
4. It is light yellow in colour but may be green or purple, and forms a mass upto 20 cm. in diameter.
5. It enters the interior of above animals and lives permanently there, forming extensive burrows and tunnels.

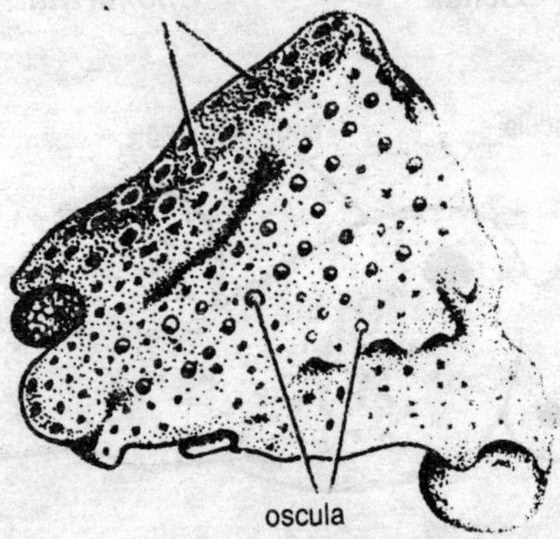

Fig. 1.8. *Cliona.*

6. Each tunnel has a raised osculum.
7. Monaxon spicules form the skeleton of the individual.
8. Sexual reproduction by the formation of gametes. Development indirect through a larval stage. The larva grows into a compact mass.
9. It has sulphurous odour hence commonly called sulphur sponge.

POTERION

The systematic position is the same as that of *Cliona.*

1. It is a solitary, marine and boring sponge.

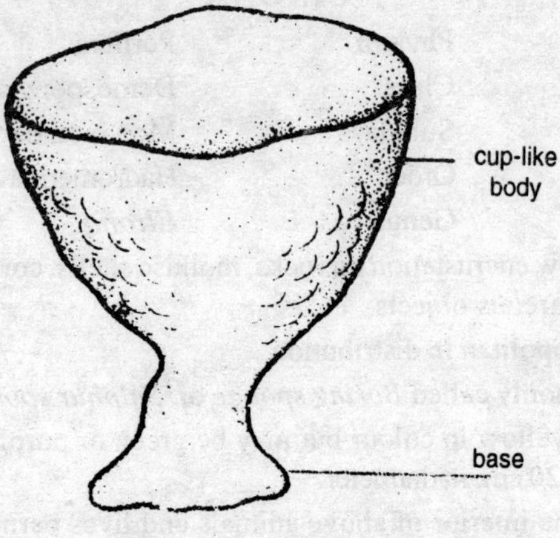

Fig. 1.9. *Poterion.*

2. It is found in the gulf of Mexico and off-coasts of North Carolina.
3. It is commonly known as *Neptune's goblet.*
4. The shape of body is cup-like with a base. The body remains fixed to the substratum by base.
5. The incurrent apertures are present on the outer surface while excurrent apertures on the inner surface.
6. The skeleton is formed of tylostyle (monaxon) spicules.
7. Osculum at the anterior end is very large.
8. It is supposed to be one of the largest sponges, measuring 1-2 metres in hight.

TETHYA

The systematic position is the same as that of *Cliona.*

1. It is a marine sponge inhibiting deep seas.
2. It is a rounded sponge.
3. Body surface tuberculate with radiating bundles of monaxon spicules and several exasters.
4. The styles have indistinct tylote ends.
5. Spongin fibres are absent.

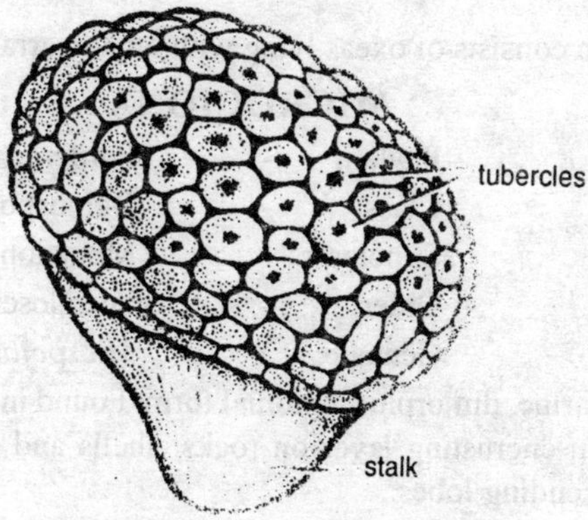

Fig. 1.10. *Tethya.*

HALICHONDRIA

Phylum	-	Porifera
Class	-	Demospongiae
Subclass	-	Monaxonida
Order	-	Halichondrina
Genus	-	*Halichondria*

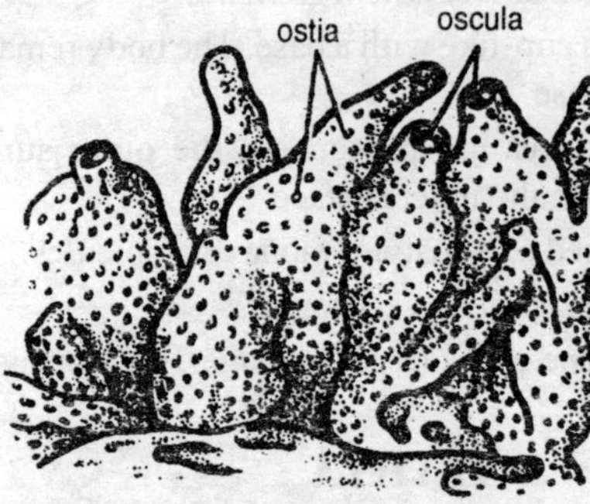

Fig. 1.11. *Halichondria.*

1. It is a colonial sponge. It forms low encrustations on rocks in shallow waters.
2. It is cosmopolitan in distribution.
3. It is commonly called the 'crumb of bread sponge'.
4. It is soft and yellowish or green or brown in colour.
5. The surface presents one or more large rounded openings called oscula.
6. Skeleton consists of oxeas lying without any arrangement.

MICROCIONA

Phylum	-	Porifera
Class	-	Demospongiae
Subclass	-	Monaxonida
Order	-	Poecilosclerina
Genus	-	*Microciona*

1. It is a marine, dimorphic, colonial form. Found in shallow water as a soft, thin encrusting layer on rocks, shells and calcareous objects with ascending lobes.
2. It is found in long Island Sound and also present in South Carolina to Cape Cod.
3. In deep sea water the colony becomes massive.
4. It is bright red in colour. The animal comprises of several finger-like projections.
5. The spicules are of various forms and united by spongin into a regularly network.

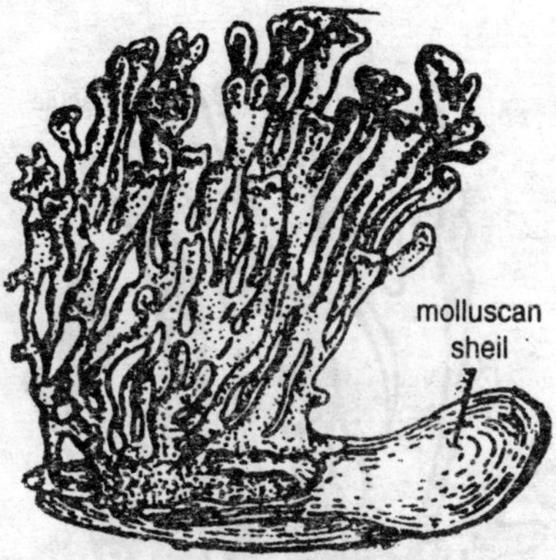

Fig. 1.12. *Microciona.*

6. The animal is used in regeneration and reassociation experiments. This animal has tremendous capacity to reassociate and regenerate.
7. Sexual reproduction by gametes. Development through a free swimming larval stage in early August.

CHALINA

Phylum	-	Porifera
Class	-	Demospongiae
Subclass	-	Monaxonida
Order	-	Haploscreina
Genus	-	*Chalina*

1. *Chalina* is commonly called *Dead man's finger* found in deep water, orange-brown or red in colour.
2. It is found in Europe, common from Rhode Island to Labrador. and North Carolina to Cape Cod.
3. It is much branched and each branch looks like a finger, so also called *Mermaid's glove*.
4. Each branch is perforated by numerous openings or oscula.
5. Canal system is *leucon type*.
6. Monaxon siliceous spicules embedded in spongin fibres constitute the skeleton of animal.
7. Asexual reproduction by budding and sexual reproduction includes a free-swimming larva.

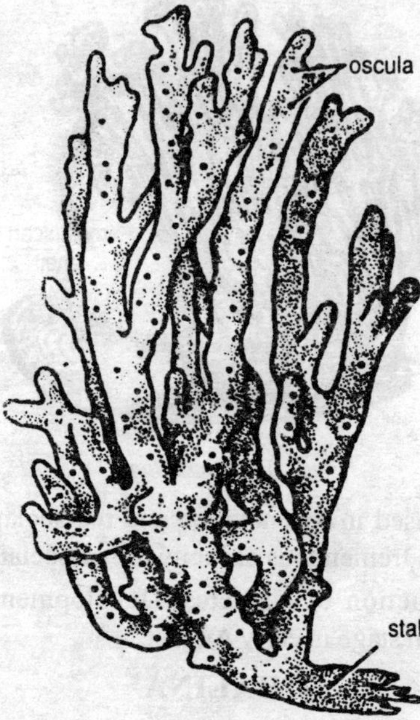

Fig. 1.13. *Chalina.*

SPONGILLA

The classification is the same as that of *Chalina.*

1. *Spongilla* is a colonial fresh-water sponge, found attached to submerged sticks and plants of ponds, lakes and streams.

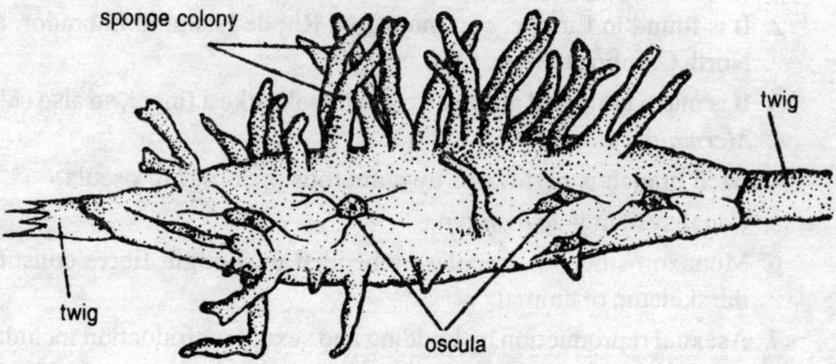

Fig. 1.14. *Spongilla.*

2. It is cosmopolitan in its distribution. It is found mainly in Atlantic, European and American waters.
3. Siliceous spicules form the skeleton. The spicules are oxeas, embedded in spongin.
4. Canal system *rhagon type*.
5. Highly branched colony with numerous oscula.
6. Asexual reproduction by budding and gemmule formation, sexual reproduction also occurs.
7. Gemmules are protected by the amphidisc spicules.

EPHYDATIA

The classification is the same as that of *Chalina*.

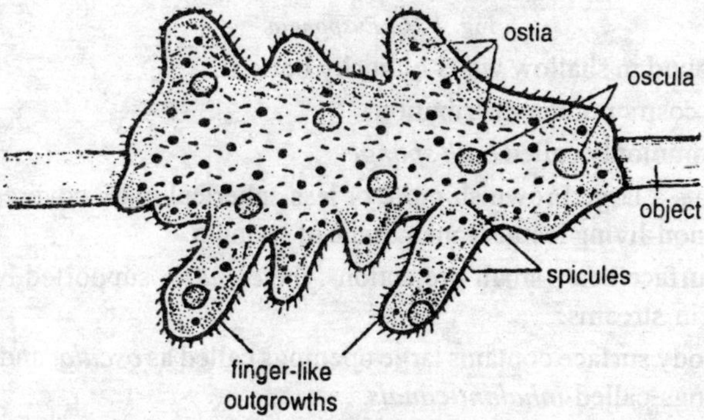

Fig. 1.15. *Ephydatia.*

1. It is a greyish or greenish fresh water sponge, found in clear water in rivers, ponds and streams.
2. It is found in Vancouver Island, Eastern and Central States.
3. The body consists of delicate tubes each bears an osculum.
4. Surface is perforated by several large oscula and minute pores, the osita.
5. The green colour of animal is due to the symbiont zoochlorellae.
6. Asexual reproduction by gemmules.

EUSPONGIA

Phylum	-	Porifera
Class	-	Demospongiae
Subclass	-	Keratosa
Genus	-	*Euspongia*

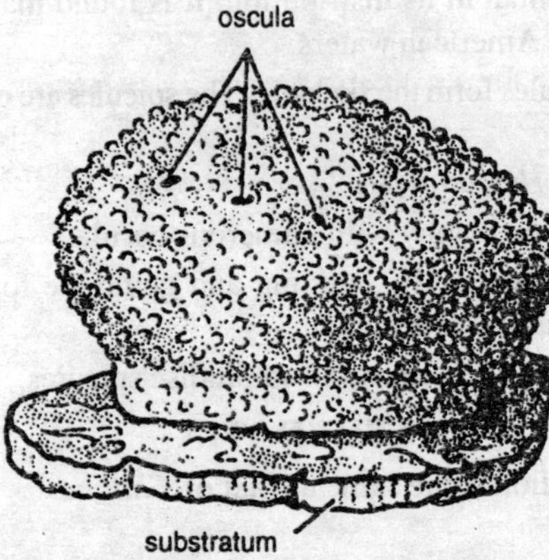

Fig. 1.16. *Euspongia.*

1. It is found in shallow water on rocky bottom.
2. It has cosmopolitan distribution.
3. It is commonly called *bath sponge.*
4. It forms a large brownish more or less spherical mass covered by a dark, non-living leathery membrane of spongin.
5. The surface bears small projections, the *conules*, supported by stiff spongin streams.
6. The body surface contains large openings called as *oscula,* and small openings called *inhalant canals.*
7. Internally the sponge resembles a liver in both consistency and colour.
8. It is unisexual and males are rare.
9. Skeleton is made of only spongin fibres. Spicules are absent. Many small worms and crustaceans live inside it as commensals.
10. It can live upto 50 years.
11. It is commonly used in bathing, washing automobiles, furnitures, applying face creams etc.

HIPPOSPONGIA

The classification is the same as that of *Euspongia.*

1. It is a horny sponge found 9-16 meters deep.
2. It is found in Mediterranean, West Indies and common in Florida.
3. Body is massive and permeated by large, often cavernonus canals.
4. Body is covered by a dark and dead membrane provided with numerous flagellated chambers.

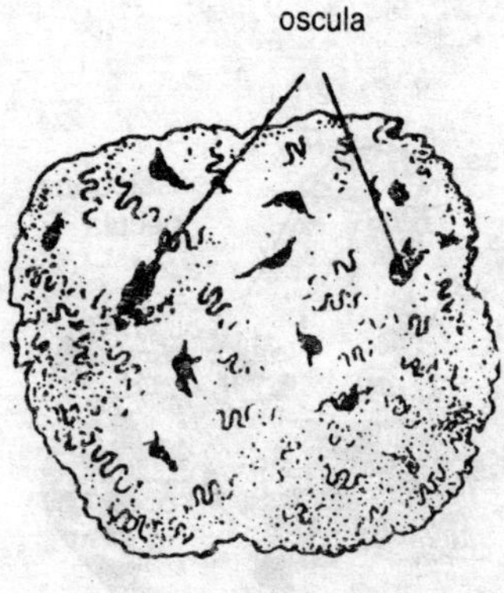

Fig. 1.17. *Hippospongia*

5. Body surface is raised at several places bearing oscula. A single sponge is made up of few to many oscula.
6. Skeleton is made up of spongin only, spicules being absent.
7. It grows very large and may live for 50 years.
8. It harbours several small commensal crustaceans and worms.

HIRCINIA

The classification is the same as that of *Euspongia.*

1. It is a marine and sedentary sponge.
2. It has world-wide distribution.
3. It is commonly called *horny sponge.*
4. It attains a considerable size and rounded massive form. Body surface contains conules.
5. The body colour is due to presence of symbiotic blue-green algae.
6. The canal system is *diplodal leucon type.*
7. Skeleton consists of spongin fibres only.

EUPLECTELLA

Phylum	-	Porifera
Class	-	Hexactinellida
Order	-	Hexasterophora
Genus	-	*Euplectella*
Species	-	*aspergillum*

1. It is a deep sea form found near Philippine islands and has become curved due to slow water current.

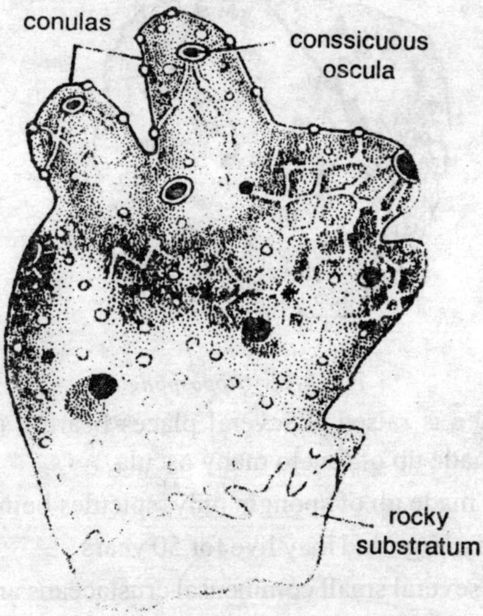

Fig. 1.18. *Hircinia.*

2. It is commonly called *Venus' flower basket* and is a beautiful glass sponge.
3. It is made of six-rayed siliceous spicules which are held together by siliceous cement resulting in a beautiful basket-like structure.

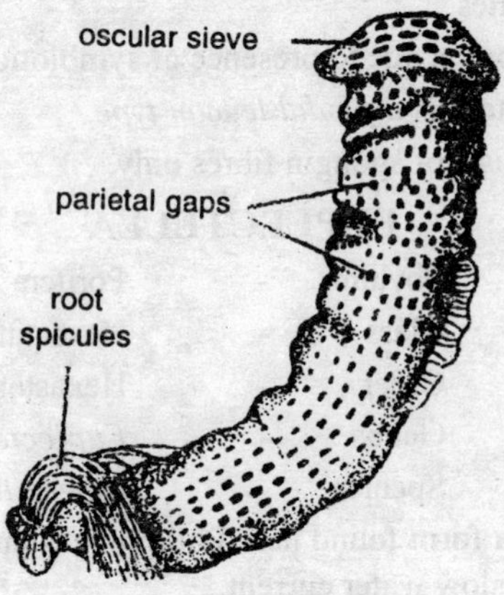

Fig. 1.19. *Euplectella.*

4. The curved upper end of the body is closed by an *oscular sieve*.
5. From the base arise root spicules which are long siliceous threads which fasten the sponge to its unstable slimy substratum.
6. The spongocoel contains a pair of crustacea (*Spongicola*) which had commensal life throughout their life. For this reason *Euplectella* is a beautiful presentation for newly married couple in Japan.

STAUROCALYPTUS

The systematic position of *Staurocalyptus* is same as that of *Euplactella*.

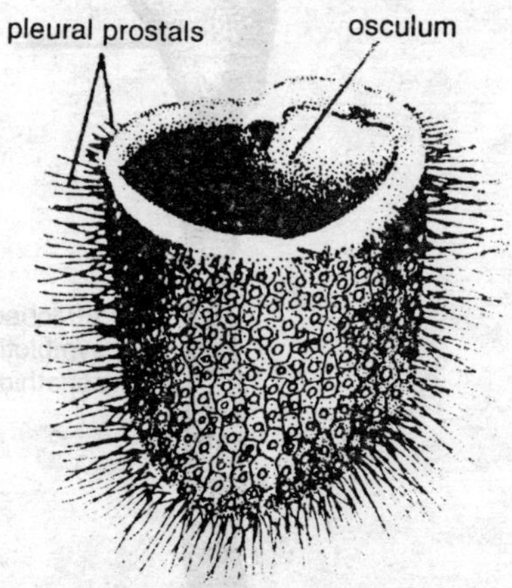

Fig. 1.20. *Staurocalyptus*.

1. *Staurocalyptus* is a marine spone and found alone i.e. *solitary*.
2. It is commonly called as *glass-sponge*.
3. The body is cup-like or sac-like without root spicules or often veiled by long projecting dermalia.
4. The skeleton is *lassacrine i.e.* the skeleton is composed of rays of large, four-rayed spicules united by cross-bars.
5. The entire body except the osculum beset with considerably long, projecting five spicules—the *pleural prostals*.
6. The spicules and threads of pure and shiny white material containing flint.
7. The osculum is considerably large.

HYALONEMA

Phylum	-	Porifera
Class	-	Hexactinellida
Order	-	Amphidiscophora
Genus	-	*Hyalonema*

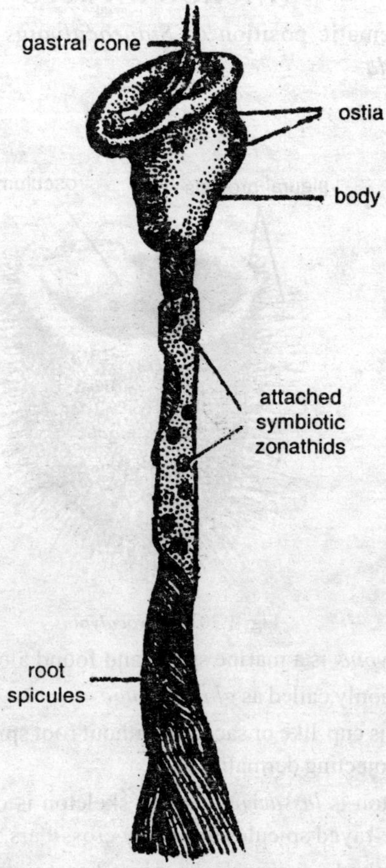

Fig. 1.21. *Hyalonema.*

1. It is a marine sponge found along new England coast.
2. It is commonly called as *glassrope sponge*.
3. It has a spherical or oval about 30 cm. long body fastened in the mud by a root-tuft of long twisted spicules.

4. The spicules continue through the body as an axis or columella and often project above it as the *gastral cone*.
5. The gastral cone bears openings of the excurrent canals.
6. The surface may be depressed to enclose a cavity, the spongocoel, or may be flat in which case there is no spongocoel and the excurrent canals open out directly.
7. It possess large amphidisc spicules like fresh-water sponges. Entire body contains small, branching, six-rayed spicules.
8. The flagellated chambers are arranged radially and in parallel planes in the sponge wall.
9. Some anemones live attached to the root-tuft and certain crustaceans live inside the body as commensals.

PHERONEMA

The classification is the same as that of *Hyalonema*.

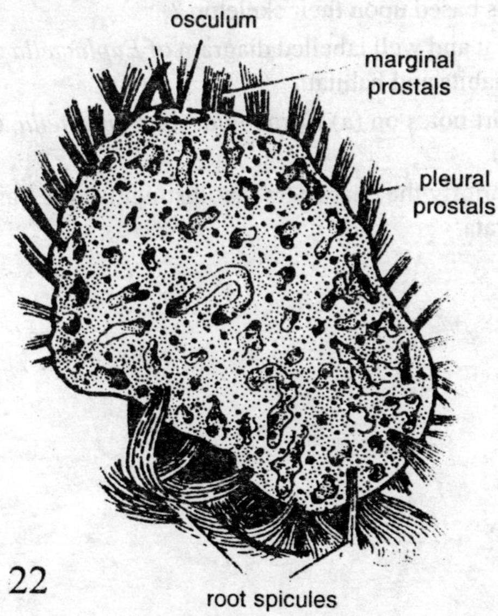

Fig. 1.22. *Pheronema*.

1. It is found on the bottom of sea. It occurs in U.K., U.S.A. and Europe.
2. It has a cup or bowl-shaped body.
3. Body thick-walled with a large spongocoel, which opens above by an osculum.
4. Osculum is guarded by spicules or *marginal* prostals.

5. Glassy spicules project from the body surface, often in tufts called the *pleural prostals,* giving the appearence of glass wool.
6. Skeleton consists of amphidisc microsclers.
7. Canal system is of *eurypylous leuconoid type*.
8. Broad, ill-defined root-tufts made of silica, which are joined and serve for attachment to the substratum.

Revision Questions

1. Give an outline classification of phylum Porifera up to orders, give examples of each order. How can you say that the classification of Porifera is based upon their skeleton ?
2. Give a neat and well labelled diagram of *Euplactella* or *Hyalonema*. Give its habits and habitat.
3. Write short notes on (a) *Euspongia,* (b) *Euplectella,* (c) *Cliona,* (d) *Spongilla.*
4. Indicate briefly the characters that distinguish the Parazoa from the Coelenterata.

2

Leucosolenia

Leucosolenia is one of the most simple sponge, growing in the sea-shore water. It belongs to the family Leucosolenidae. It is an asconoid sponge which resembles very much with the olynthus stage, found in the life cycle of certain other sponges like *Scypha*; as such it is also referred to as *olynthus-type*. Near about 100 species have been recorded uptil now, out of which *L. complicata*, *L. botryoides,* and *L. variabilis* are quite common. The description given below is the general one and is applicable to all the species.

SYSTEMATIC POSITION

Phylum	-	Porifera
Class	-	Calcarea
Order	-	Homocoela
Genus	-	*Leucosolenia*

Habitat

Leucosolenia is a small delicate, branching, colonial marine sponge. It occurs almost all over the world in shallow water below low tide mark on rocks, stones and warfs. It does not live in calm water but is found abundenty where wave action is intense. The wave action ensures adequate food supply and well-oxygenated water. There are about 100 species but the common species are *L.botryoides, L.complicate* and *L.variabilis.*

Habits

Leucosolenia is a colonial sponge. The colony is permanently fixed to the substratum. It feeds on microscopic animals, plants and organic particles. Digestion is intracellular as in Protozoa. Reproduction occurs both asexually and sexually. Life-history includes a free-swimming flagellated larva for dispersal. The sponge is very sensitive to external conditions and dies if removed from its habitat. It has a good degree of power of regeneration.

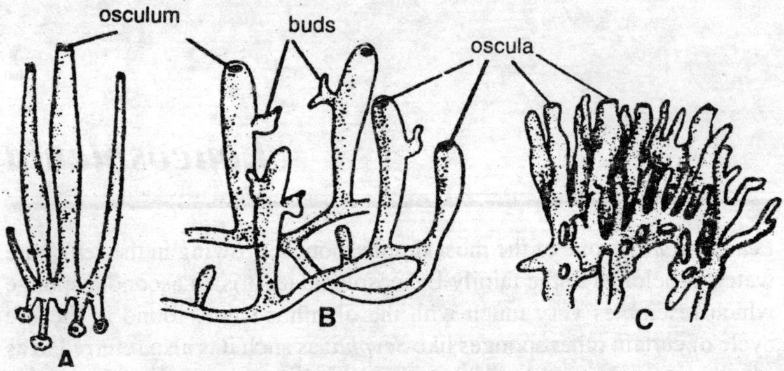

Fig. 2.1. Types of *Leucosolenia*. A—Simple, B—Branching. C—Reticulate.

Structure

Shape and size. The colonies of *Leucosolenia* consist of numerous cylindrical structures each of which is a complete animal. It is a radially symmetrical animal. All the cylinders of the colony are attached to each other at the base due to which the colony appears as a thick branched bush-like structure. Each cylinder is about 25 mm long and whitish or yellowish in colour.

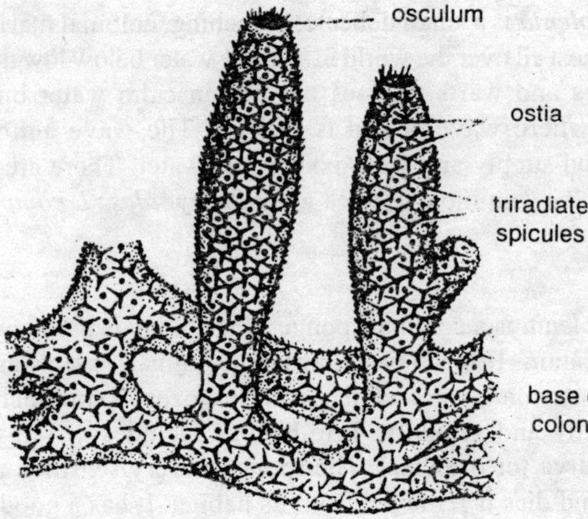

Fig. 2.2. *Leucosolenia*. A part of the colony.

The cylinders of *Leucosolenia* are radially symmetrical thin walled tubes which represent the *Olynthus stage*. In the centre of each cylinder is a cavity called *spongocoel* which opens to the outside by a large aperture known as *osculum*. The wall of the cylinder is perforated by numerous pores which are intracellular and called *incurrent pores* or *ostia*. They lead into the spongocoel.

The *porocytes* are extremely elastic and close the ostia by contracting. The water current reaches the spongocoel through the ostia. The spongocoel is lined with choanocytes. The water of the spongocoel is expelled out through the *osculum* by the movement of the flagella of choanocytes, therefore, the structure of *Leucosolenia* is very simple.

BODY WALL

The body wall is thin with an outer epidermis or *pinacoderm* and inner endodermis or *choanoderm* with a non-cellular mesenchyme or mesogloea in between. The wall is perforated by Pinacocytes numerous pores through which water enters the spongocoel and passes out through osculum.

1. Pinacoderm

The outer layer consists of a single layer of thin, scale-like, flattened cells called the *Pinacocytes*. The cells have thin margins and a bulging central part with a nucleus. The margins show contractility so that the sponge can increase or decrease in size to some extent.

Specially, large and tubular *porocytes* are also present which are supposed to be modified pinacocytes. Each porocytes has a central canal-like space which communicates with the exterior through ostia or dermal pores. Internally, they open into the spongocoel. The ostia are regulated by myocytes which form circlets around the openings.

2. Choanoderm

It consists of a single layer of flagellated cells or choanocytes which line the spongocoel. A choanocyte cell resembles the choanoflagellate protozoa. It is an ovoid cell, its free end bearing a transparent contractile collar which surrounds a single long flagellum arising from a basal granule. The nucleus lies at the centre of the cell. These cells are used in feeding and for ensuring the flow of water within the animal's body.

3. Mesenchyme or Mesohyl

Mesenchyme lies between pinacoderm and choanoderm. It is a thin gelatinous layer secreted by the choanocytes and holds the spicules in space. Within the mesenchyme lie freely wandering amoeba-like, *amoebocytes* and the spicules.

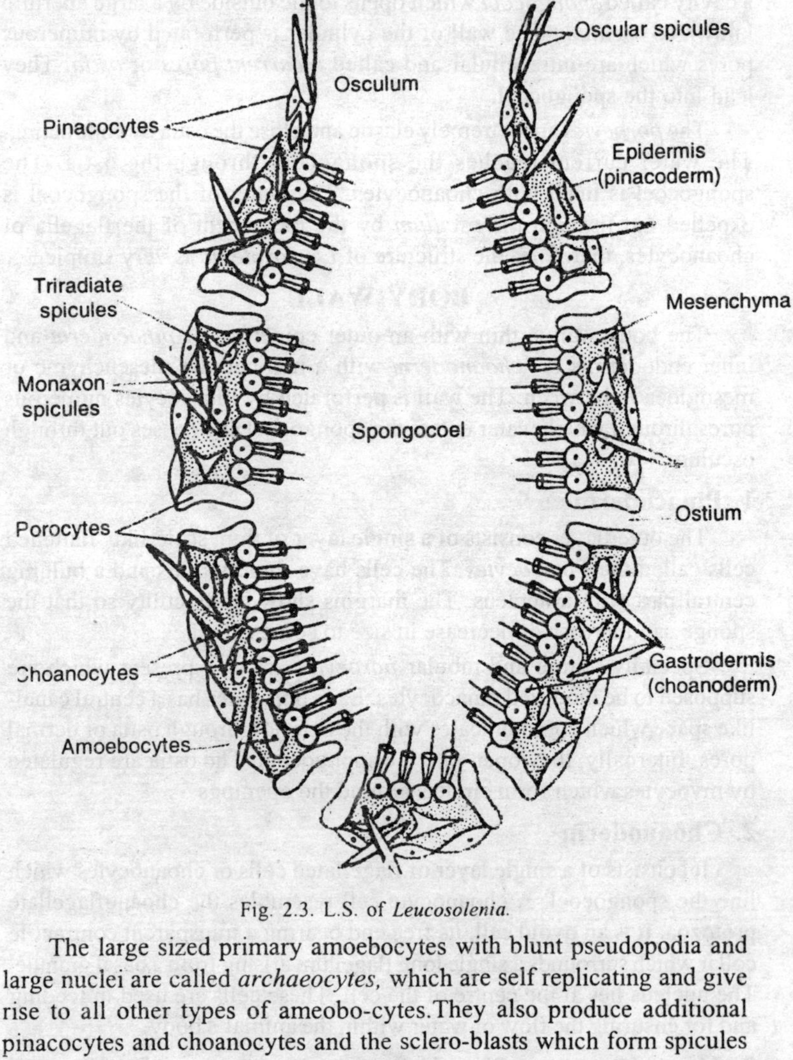

Fig. 2.3. L.S. of *Leucosolenia.*

The large sized primary amoebocytes with blunt pseudopodia and large nuclei are called *archaeocytes,* which are self replicating and give rise to all other types of ameobo-cytes.They also produce additional pinacocytes and choanocytes and the sclero-blasts which form spicules and the reproductive cells. The archaeocytes carry on all the physiological activities of the sponge.

The spicules, formed of crystalline calcium carbonate, may be needle-shaped mono-axons or tetraxons with four rays and triaxons with three rays. The spicules are embedded in the mesohyl but protrude out of the body to give roughness.

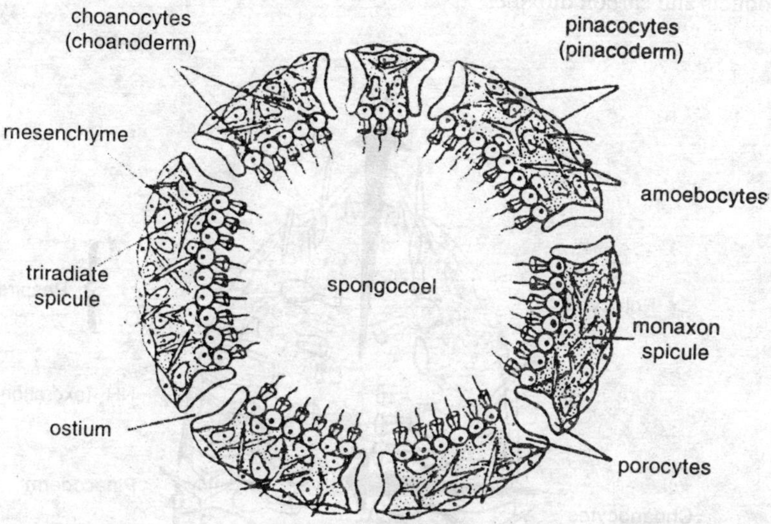

Fig. 2.4. *Leucosolenia* T.S.

PHYSIOLOGY

The sponges being fixed animals are quiet and inactive-looking animals. Their physiology is mainly drawing a current of sea-water into their bodies.

The movement of the flagella of collar cells create the force, which draws a current of sea-water through the numerous dermal ostia into the spongocoel. The current brings with it minute organisms that constitute the food of the sponge. Flagellum of the collar cell stirs the food particles , which slowly settle down on the surface of the collar and over its basal part. Small pseudopodia-like processes of the basal part engulf the particles and form food vacuoles.Part or whole of the digestion takes place in the basal part and the products of digestion are then passed on the amoeboid cells of the mesohyl, where digestion is completed. Digested food is transported to other parts of the body as the mesohyl cells move away. Amoebocytes pick up food particles directly. Such amoebocytes are located along the course of the canals in higher sponges. Undigestible material is thrown off into the spongo-coel or into the space within the collar. Food is stored by specified amoebocytes termed *thesocytes*.

Water current not only brings food with it but also maintains a supply of fresh and oxygenated water. Oxygen diffuses into the cells with which the sea-water comes in contact. The water current leaves the spongocoel through the osculum and carries with it undigestible material, excretory products and carbon dioxide.

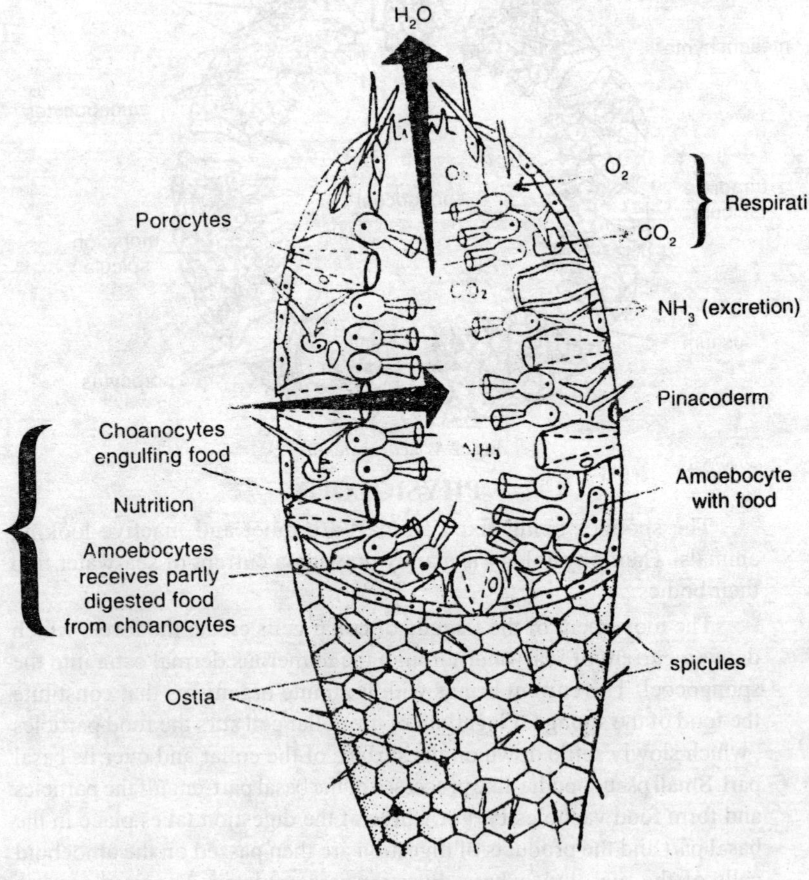

Fig. 2.5. Flow of water through the body.

Sponges do not have nerve cells or sensory cells but are able to respond to the changes in salinity illumination and mechanical contact.

Nutrition

The food of the animal comprises the microscopic animals, plants, and organic particles which are taken into the spongocoel along with the water and captured by the choanocytes from the moving water. In the choanocytes the food is partially digested and then this food is passed on to amoebocytes i.e. trophocytes where complete digestion takes place. These cells then distribute the digested food from cell to cell. Digestive enzymes, however, are more common in the choanocytes than they are in the amoebocytes *(Hartman, 1960)*. Egested waste is dropped by the amoebocytes into the water current.

Respiration and Excretion

Gaseous exchange of oxygen and carbon dioxide occurs between the amoebocytes, choanocytes and pinacocytes and the water flowing through the canal system. Similarly nitrogenous wastes are avoided.

Locomotion

The sponges are fixed, as such they are incapable of movement However, the porocytes can be opened and closed according to the needs, and the amoebocytes can also move freely within the mesenchyme.

Behaviour

There is no coordinating nervous system in the animal.The individual cell responds independently to the external stimuli. The flagella of the choanocytes beat constantly to create a water current. Osculum may close independently without altering the activities of other structures. Induced prolonged contraction may cause the sponge to burst, indicating little co-ordination.

REPRODUCTION

Leucosolenia reproduces both by asexual and sexual means.

(a) Asexual reproduction

Asexual reproduction takes place by *external budding*. Small outgrowths, called the *buds,* arise from the sides of the erect branches as well as from the upper surface of the horizontal branches. The buds grow and, after attaining sufficient size, acquire osculum at their top, thus forming new individuals. The latter may remain attached to the parent colony and add to its size or become free by death and decay of old parts and form new colonies.

(b) Sexual reproduction

The sexual reproduction occurs by sperms and ova. Gamete formation and fertilization are similar in *Leucosolenia* and *Scypha* and will be described in the latter.

Zygote undergoes *holoblastic cleavage* and gives rise to an oval embryo called the *coeloblastula*. The latter is composed of a single layer of columnar flagellated cells with a few rounded, granular, non-flagellated cells at the posterior pole. The non-flagellated cells are thought to be the archaeocytes which will produce all future archaeocytes of the sponge. Some adjacent flagellated cells lose flagelia and also migrate into the cavity. The embryo now consists of an outer layer of flagellated cells and an inner mass of amoeboid cells. It is known as the *stereogastrula* or *parenchymula*. It makes its way into the spongocoel and escapes through the osculum into the surrounding water, thus becoming a free-swimming larva.

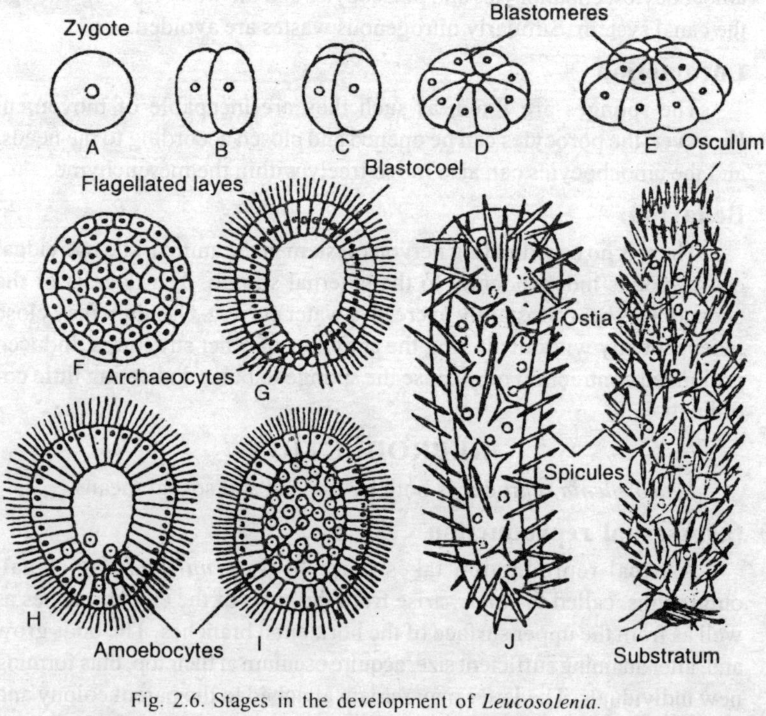

Fig. 2.6. Stages in the development of *Leucosolenia*.

The *parenchymula* larva swims about freely for a few hours, going away from the parent sponge. Finally, it fixes itself to some object by its anterior pole and flattens out. The internal amoebocytes migrate to the exterior and spread out to form a dermal layer or epidermis and mesenchyme. The flagellated cells, which get enclosed by the epidermis, change into choanocytes. A central cavity or spongocoel appears and gets lined by choanocytes. An osculum breaks through at the top and incurrent pores or ostia appear in the porocytes that differentiate in the wall of the sponge by this time. Scleroblasts shift from the epidermis into the mesenchyme and start secreting spicules. This results in a small sponge and takes only a few days.

Revision Questions

1. Give an account of the structure, physiology and reproduction of an asconoid sponge studied by you.
2. Draw a labelled sketch of the L.S. of *Leucosolenia.* Description is not required.
3. Describe the structure and life history of *Leucosolenia.*
4. Write short notes on (a) Osculum, (b) Coeloblastula, (c) Pinacoderm, (d) Choanoderm.

3

Scypha (Sycon)

SYSTEMATIC POSITION

Phylum	-	Porifera
Class	-	Calcarea
Order	-	Heterocoela
Genus	-	*Scypha (Sycon)*

Habits and Habitat

Scypha is more complex than *Leucosolenia. Leucosolenia* shows primitive asconoid type of structure while in *Scypha,* there is folding of body wall to show syconoid type of structure where the spongocoel is reduced. *Scypha* is a small, marine sponge found attached by a sticky secretion to some submerged solid objects like rocks, shells of molluscs and corals. It is found in shallow water upto a depth of 100 meters where waves provide the animal with plenty of food and well oxygenated water. It has many species and is widely distributed but is best, known from North Atlantic shores. It may be solitary but also forms a cluster or colony by budding.

External Morphology

Scypha or *Sycon* possesses a vase-shaped and radially symmetrical body which measures from 1 to 3 cm. in length. The colour is not specific but varies from grey to light brown. Near the attached end are found a few small tubular projections, or the *buds,* which are formed not so extensively as in *Leucosolenia* or other asconoid sponges. The free end of the vase-shaped individual bears an opening, the *osculum* (*exhalent* or *excurrent pore*), which is fringed with long, straight, needle-like monaxon spicules. This *oscular fringe* checks small animals from entering into the body. The body surface is thrown into regularly arranged polygonal elevations from which project spear-like spicules, called *oxeotes* (monaxon spicules) that impart a bristly appearance to the body. The polygonal

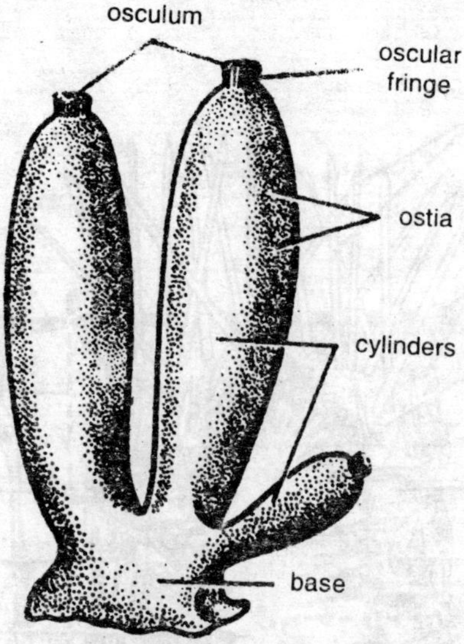

Fig. 3.1. *Scypha* (*Sycon*).

elevations are separated by deep grooves, bearing minute pores, i.e. , the *ostia,* which lead into the central body cavity, the *spongocoel* or *paragastric cavity*, through a system of canals.

CANAL SYSTEM

As in other sponges, *Scypha* has the peculiarity of having canal system which consists of complex system of pores and canals. The body is traversed by numerous canals of several types. The body wall is thick and folded so as to form regularly arranged alternating invagi-nations and evaginations, forming sycon type of canal system. The different components of canal system of *Sycon* are given below.

1. Ostia or Dermal Pores

The external large openings of the incurrent canals are stretched over a thin membrane, called the *pore-membrane*. It bears two or more openings for the ingress of outside water into the body of sponge. These pores are known as *ostia* (L., *ostium*, door) or *dermal pores*. Because of the presence of contractile cells, the *myocytes*, around them the ostia can reduce in diameter and thus regulate the amount of ingressing water.

2. Incurrent canals

The incurrent canals are narrow and almost squarish in cross-section. They end blindly at their inner extremities, a little distance away from the

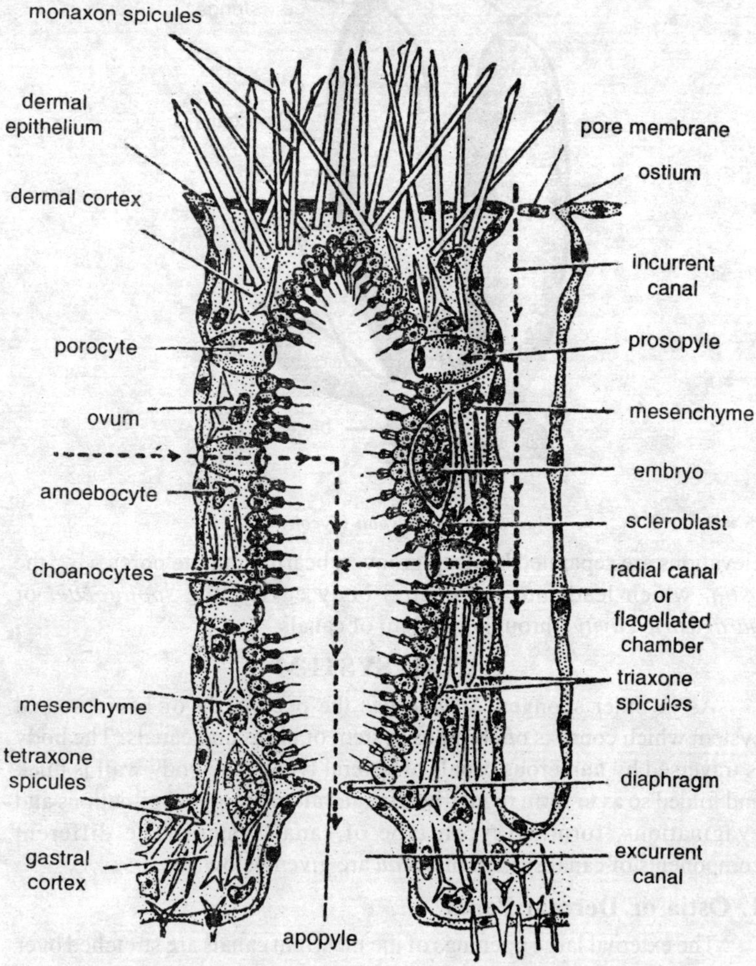

Fig. 3.2. A part of verticle section of *Scypha* showing histology and canal system.

spongocoel. Externally they become somewhat dilated. The dilated part of each canal is closed externally by a thin pore-membrane that bears 3 or 4 minute openings, the *dermal ostia,* already referred to. The pore membrane also contains myocytes, some of which surround the dermal ostia and serve to close them when necessary. The incurrent canals are lined by flat pinacocytes similar to those lining the spongocoel.

3. Prosopyles

The incurrent canals are communicated with the radial canals through intercellular spaces, called *prosopyles* (Gr., *Pros*, near+*pyle*, gate). Some authors are of view that in the young *Sycon* these openings are those of the porocytes, as in *Leucosolenia*, but in adult the porocytes degenerate leaving the empty spaces or the prosopyles

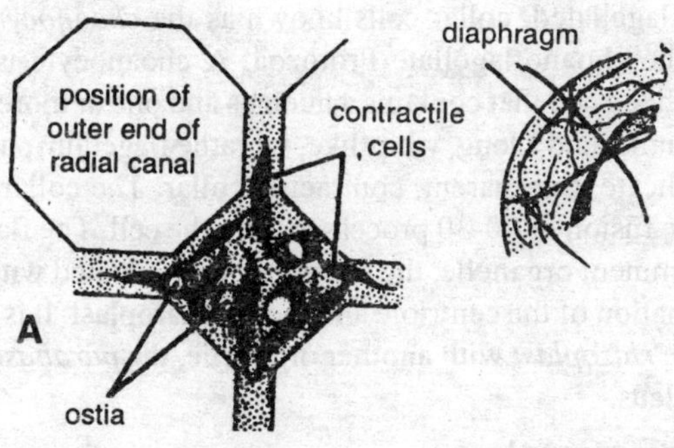

Fig. 3.3. Apopyle lined by myocytes in *Scypha*.

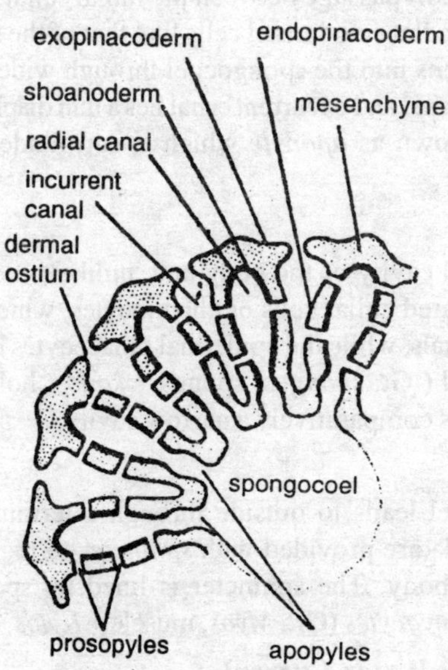

Fig. 3.4. A portion of a T.S. of *Scypha*.

4. Radial canals

The radial canals are relatively wide and are polygonal in cross-section. They are closed at their outer ends which lie some distance inside the polygonal surface elevations. Internally they open into the excurrent canals by apertures called *apopyles*. An apopyle is a large circular opening in the center of a thin partition, the *diaphragm*, that stretches between the adjoining radial and excurrent canals. It can be contracted or dilated by myocytes that border it. The radial canals are lined by a layer of loosely arranged, flagellated, collar cells known as the *choanocytes*. The latter resemble the choanoflagellate Protozoa. A choanocyte is a somewhat oval or rounded cell that contains a nucleus and one or more vacuoles and bears at its inner end a long, whip-like, vibratile flagellum partly surrounded by a delicate, transparent, contractile collar. The collar is formed by side-to-side fusion of 20-30 processes from the cell. The flagellum arises from a prominent organelle, the *blepharoplast,* situated within the cell. It is a combination of the centriole and the blepharoplast. It is connected by a thread the *rhizoplast* with another organelle, the *parabasal body*, lying on the nucleus.

5. Excurrent canals

Each excurrent canal leads the radial canal into the spongocoel and forms a wide and short passage between the radial canal and spongocoel. These are lined with flat ectodermal cells like that of the spongocoel. The excurrent canal opens into the spongocoel through wide gastrial ostium. Between the radial canal and excurrent canal lies a thin diaphragm perforated by a large hole known as *apopyle* which is surrounded by contractile myocytes.

6. Spongocoel

It is the central cavity of the body and, unlike *Leucosolenia*, is not lined by the flagellated collar cells or choanocytes, which have departed to line the radial canals, while the epidermal pinacocytes have immigrated into the spongocoel (Gr, *spongos*, spongs + *koilos,* hollow) to form its lining. This cavity is comparatively a narrow cavity.

7. Osculum

The spongocoel leads to outside through a terminal opening, the *osculum.* The oscula are provided with *sphincter* to regulate the rate of water flow in the body. The sphincter is lined by special contractile pinacocytes called *myocytes* (Gr., *Myos*, muscle + *Kytos*, cell).

Physiology of the Water Current

The flagella of the collar cells beat without coordination yet maintain a steady current of water flowing in the sponge from outside. The current enters the pores in the pore-membrane of the incurrent canals and fills the latter, it then passes into the flagellated canals through the prosopyles. From here it goes into the excurrent canals by way of apopyles. Finally, the current is thrown into the spongocoel by the large gastrial ostia from where it escapes through the osculum. The osculum is also surrounded by myocytes serving to form an *oscular sphincter,* which can close the osculum.

The course taken by water into the canal system is as under :

Water from outside —through dermal ostia→ incurrent canals —through prosopyles→ radial canals —through apopyles→ Excurrent canal → spongocoel —through osculum→ Outside

Significance of canal system

The water current flowing through the canal system brings with it food in the form of micro-organisms and oxygen. The food, chiefly unicellular alage, bacteria and organic microfragments, is collected by the collar cells just the same way as described for *Leucosolenia.* The out going current carries with it undigestible wastes carbon dioxide and nitrogenous excreta.

CELLULAR ORGANIZATION

Studies on structure and morphogenesis of *Scypha* have clearly revealed the presence of two types of cellular layers, the *pinacoderm* and the *choanoderm* with an intermediate mesenchyme.The former controls the interrelations between the mesenchyme and the external medium, while the choanoderm controls mainly the nutrition of the animal.

1. Pinacoderm

The pinacoderm comprises (i) the *exopinacoderm* (dermal epithelium) covering the entire body surface except the dermal ostia and osculum and (ii) the *endopinacoderm* which includes the epithelial lining of the incurrent canals and spongocoel. The pinacoderm is composed of large, flattened, polygonal cells, the *pinacocytes* (Gr., *pinako*, plank + *kytos*, cell). In profile, these cells present a central bulging containing the nucleus. The margins of adjacent cells are closely cemented together. Pinacocytes are highly contr-actile and they can greatly increase or reduce the surface area of the sponge body.

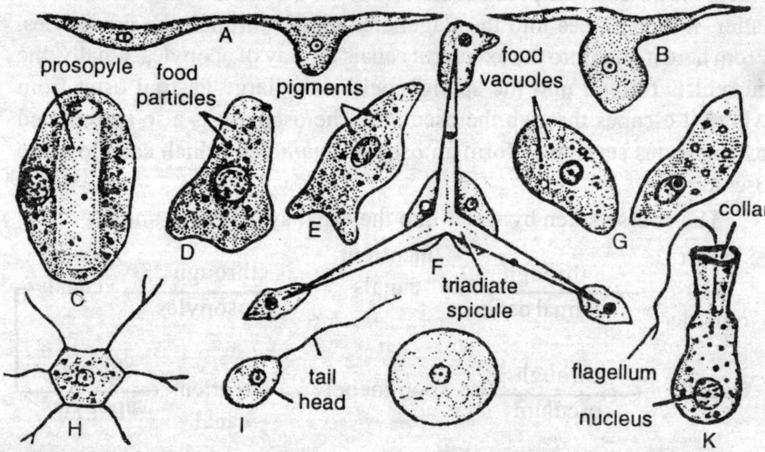

Fig. 3.5. *Scypha.* Kinds of cells. A—Pinacocyte. B—Myocyte. C—Porocyte. D—Thesocyte. E—Chromocyte. F—Sclerocytes. G—Archaeocytes. H—Collencyte. I—Sperm. J—Ovum. K—Choanocyte.

In the lining of the incurrent canals, some of the pinacocytes are modified to form tubular cells, the *poro-cytes*, connecting the incurrent canals with the radial canals through their intracellular channels, the *prosopyles*. The porocytes are thin-walled cells, open at both ends and with the nucleus present in the peripheral cytoplasm. As has already been noted, the porocytes in the adult sponge are lacking altogether. Pinacocytes surrounding the osculum, outer or dermal ostia and inner ostia or apopyles are elongated and contractile and act as muscle cells, called the *myocytes*. They form the sphincters around them to regulate their openings.

2. Choanoderm

This is the endoderm that forms the gastric epithelium and consists of flagellated collar cells or *choanocytes.* They are oval or rounded cells arranged upon the mesenchyme. Each cell contains a single nucleus, one or two contractile vacuoles, food vacuoles, reserve food, parabasal body, rhizoplast and a single basal granule or kinetosome from which whip-like flagellum arises. The flagellum is surrounded at its base by a thin cytoplasmic collar. The flagellum has two central fibrils and nine double peripheral fibrils. The collar of the flagellum is contractile and is made up of a ring of erect and closely set microvilli which project from the cell. The choanocytes line the radial canals or flagellated chambers. The movement of these flagella causes a current of water.

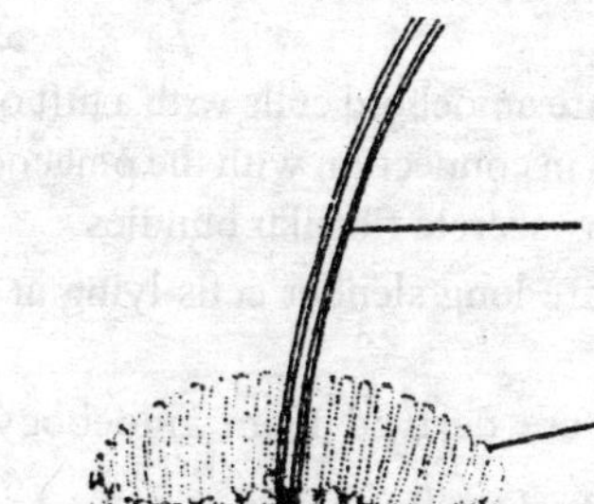

Fig. 3.6. Ultrastructure of Choanocyte.

3. Mesenchyme

The mesenchyme which fills the space between the two body layers is composed of as thin gelatinous matrix which contains many kinds of amoeboid cells such as:

(i) *Collencytes*–Star-shaped cells which are sometimes united to form a network.

(ii) *Chromocytes*– Pigmented cells with lobose pseudopodia. They probably impart colour to the sponge.

(iii) *Thesocytes*– Cells with lobose pseudopodia and are laden with reserve food material.

(iv) *Scleroblasts*–These secrete the spicules.

(v) *Trophocytes*– They are loaded with partly or completely digested food. They serve to transfer food from one place to another.

(vi) *Phagocytes*– These cells collect food from the choanocytes through their pseudopodia and also engulf excreta and damaged tissues.

(vii) *Archaeocytes*– or undifferentiated embryonic cells that give rise to sex cells.

(viii) *Lophocytes*– These are amoeboid cells with a tuft of fibrils at one or both ends and occurs in connection with the pinacocyte. Its function is unknown but it may secrete fibrillar bundles.

(ix) *Desmocytes*– They are long slender cells lying at the basement of the canals.

(x) *Gland cells*– They are derived from amoebocytes and secrete mucous.

(xi) *Germ cells*– Some of the amoebocytes (archaeocytes) differentiate into sex cells i.e. ova or sperms. However, in some sponges, they are said to be modified choanocytes.

(xii) *Myocytes*–Around the apopyles, osculum, and ostia are present a number of narrow elongated highly contractile cells, the *myocytes*.

The mesenchyme also contains the spicules which are monaxonic and triradiate in form. These serve to strengthen the body and hold it up right.

SKELETON

The skeleton of *Sycon* consists of calcareous spicules having crystalline appearance which supports and protects the soft parts. They have an axis of organic material around which is deposited the inorganic substance i.e. calcium carbonate or hydrated silica. The spicules are secreted by sclerocyte cells and each ray of the spicule is said to be secreted by two such cells.The sclerocytes are in their turn produced by scleroblast cells. Spicules of *Sycon* show a variety of shapes and sizes and have a particular arrangement with regard to their canal system.The following are the main types of spicules:

(i) Large single rayed, needle-shaped *monaxon spicules* arranged in a circlet around the osculum, (ii) Simple *spear-like monaxon* spicules projecting from dermal cortex opposite the outer ends of the radial canals, (iii) Triaxon or three rayed spicules are present along the radial canals with their one end pointing towards the distal ends of the canals, (iv) Four rayed, *tetraxon spicules* are present in the thick gastral cortex alongwith triaxon spicules and surround the spongocoel. Thus the long monaxons surround the osculum in the form of oscular fringe while the short monaxons lie parallel to the radial canals. The triradiates mostly lie along the radial canals with one ray facing externally. The tetraradiate spicules also lie in the same region.

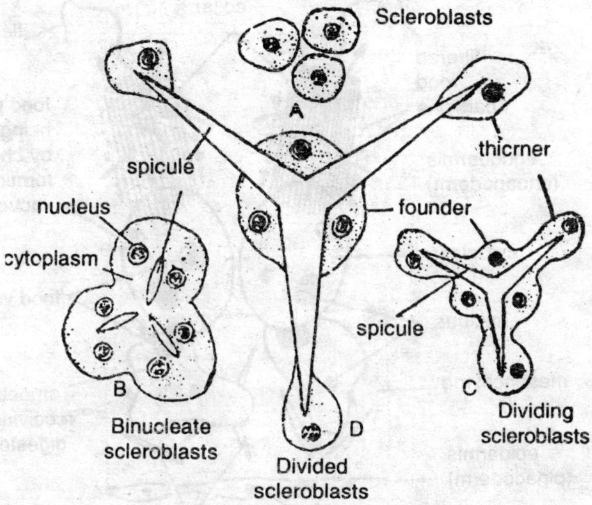

Fig. 3.7. Secretion of triradiate spicules

NUTRITION

Nutritionally, *Scypha* is both holozoic and saprozoic. Its food consists of microscopic organisms, organic debris and *detritus*.

Ingestion takes place in an interesting way. The ceaseless, though uncoordinated , beating of the flagella of the choanocytes set up a water current that draws the food particles into the radial canals through the dermal ostia, incurrent canals and prosopyles. The flagellum undulates from the base to the tip and this creates a current that starts from the base of the flagellum and passes towards its tip. This in turn draws the food particles towards the collar, because it surrounds the base of the flagellum and here they adhere to its outer sticky surface. These particles are then engulfed by pseudopodia arising from the choanocyte at the base of its collar.

Digestion in *Scypha* is completely intracellular and occurs in food vacuoles in much the same way in Protozoa. Enzymes secreted in the food-vacuoles by the surrounding cytoplasm gradually digest the food. Contents of the vacuoles are first acidic and later become alkaline. This corresponds to the acidic phase of digestion in the stomach and alkaline phase in the intestine of higher animals. All the 3 types of enzymes, viz, *proteases, carbohydrases* and *lipases,* have been isolated, but it is not certain whether they are secreted by *Scypha* itself or by bacteria that about in it.

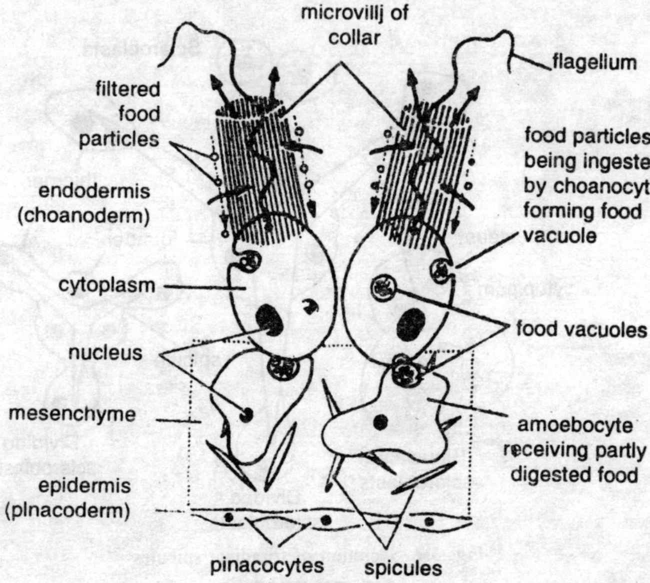

Fig 3.8. *Scypha.* Feeding mechanism and digestion of food.

Distribution of digested food to other cells (pinacocytes, myocytes, etc.) is affected in two ways: by cell to cell diffusion and by amoebocytes, called *trophocytes*, that take up wholly or partly digested food from the choanocytes and move about in the mesenchyme delivering nutrient to various cells.

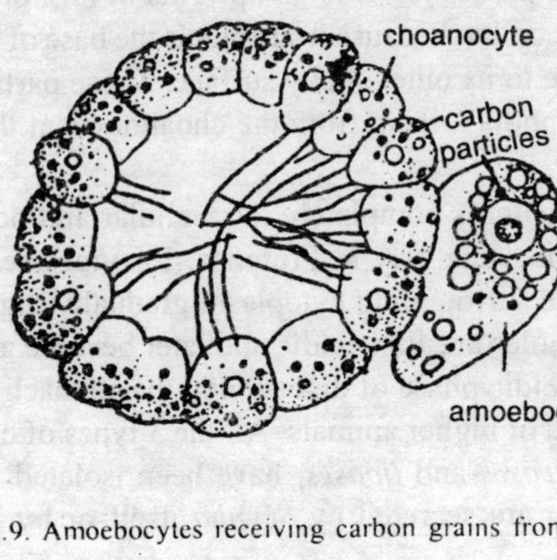

Fig. 3.9. Amoebocytes receiving carbon grains from choanocytes.

Storage of food occurs in certain amoebocytes, called *thesocytes*, in the form of glycogen, fat, glycoprotein or lipoprotein.

Egestion is brought about by choanocytes and amoebocytes that throw off indigestible pieces into the canals, from where they are ultimately driven out through the osculum by the outgoing current of water.

SENSITIVITY

Sponges do not have a nervous system and their responses are mainly local. The osculum is the most sensitive part, it collapses when the incoming current is polluted, or a strong beam of light is focussed over it or, when the sponge is partly submerged or is touched by some object. It seems that under the influence of a stimulus myocytes contract causing the closure of the osculum. The stimulus then gradually passes down the cylinder for a short distance probably by means of the mesh of neurons. Myocytes are probably *neuromuscular cells.* Occurrence of bipolar and multipolar nerve-cell, the *neurons*, has been claimed by *M.P. de Ceccatty* (1955) in the mesohyl beneath the dermal membrane of certain sponges. In a few species of Demospongiae and Calcarea *lophocytes* are believed to serve a sensory function (*W.C. Jones,* 1962). Whether or not, there are nerve-cells in sponges, their responses are so simple that one sometimes doubts the necessity of nerve cells. For instance, a sponge named *Oscarella lobularis* responds to varying light intensities; it becomes deep red in light and turns brown in dark. The significance of this change is unknown, but it occurs slowly and does not seem to be controlled by

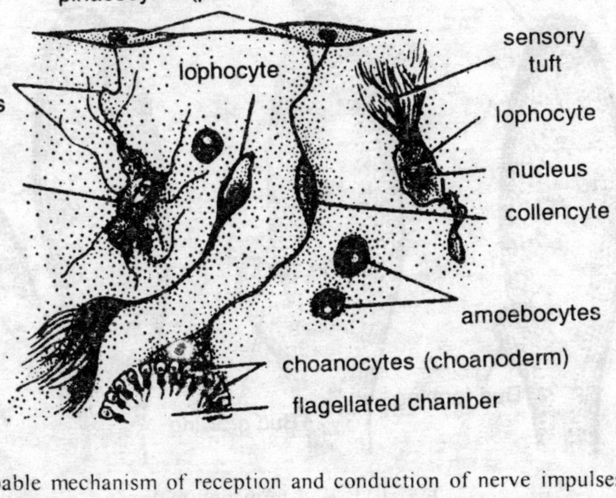

Fig. 3.10. Probable mechanism of reception and conduction of nerve impulses in a sponge.

nerve cells. Similarly many sponges secrete lot of slime when lifted out of water. It is perhaps a direct response of pinacocytes at the surface to a change in their environment. It does not call for a nervous system.

Respiration

Respiration is aerobic and is accomplished externally by the general body surface or pinacocytes and internally by choanocytes and lining cells. Each cell respires for itself, oxygen entering the cell and carbon dioxide leaving the cell by simple diffusion. Amoebocytes distribute oxygen within the mesenchyme and carry away carbon dioxide. The entire process is again intracellular.

Excretion

The nitrogenous waste is ammonia for most part and in all probability it leaves the cell by diffusion. It has also been claimed by some investigators that the nitrogenous wastes first are taken up by the amoebocytes which are then discharged into the spongocoel, from where they pass out in the water current through osculum.

REPRODUCTION

Scypha reproduces asexually as well as sexually as given below :

1. Asexual Reproduction

(i) *Budding :* It is a very common method of asexual reproduction. Masses of archaeocytes migrate to the tips of spicules clumps that project

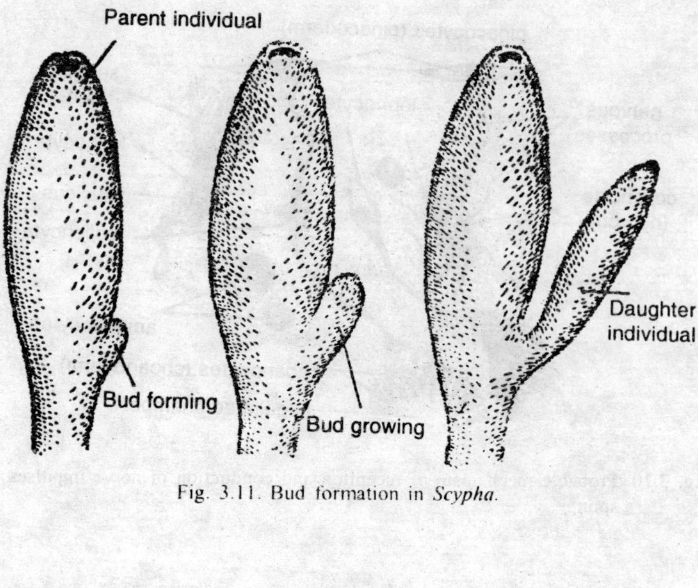

Fig. 3.11. Bud formation in *Scypha*.

from the surface in the form of bud. These buds either remain attached and grow in size, thus increasing the bulk of the sponge or it may finally breaks up and form new sponge.

(ii) *Regeneration :* Regeneration is the power to replace the parts lost by injury. The power of regeneration has developed to such an extent that if a sponge is thoroughly teared or squeezed in the sea water so as to separate the cells from one another, it is found that the cells slowly come together and gradually form a young sponge again.

2. Sexual reproduction

Scypha is a *monoecious* sponge but due to *protogyny*, only cross-fertilization occurs. Special sex organs are lacking. Male sex cells, the *sperms* and the female sex cells, the *ova* , are found in the mesenchyme. They develop from undifferentiated amoebocytes, called *archaeocytes.*

(a) Spermatogenesis. The sperm mother cell or *spermatogonium* is said to be an enlarged archaeocyte. However, it is supposed to be a modified choanocyte by *Gatenby*, who described the transformation of an entire flagellated chamber into spermatozoa. Soon the spermatogonium is surrounded by one or more flattened cover cells to form the *spermatocyst.* The cover cells are derived either by the division of the mother cell or from other amoebocytes. The spermatogonium undergoes two or three divisions to form the spermatocytes which give rise to *spermatozoa*. A mature sperm or *spermatozoon* consists of a rounded, nucleated head and vibratile tail, by the lashing movements of which it moves in water to reach other sponges.

(b) *Oogenesis*. The egg mother cell or *oogonium* is derived from large archaeocyte with a distinct nucleus. This may sometimes arise by transformation of a choanocyte which store some food, loses its flagellum and sinks into the amoebocyte and grows by engulfing other cells which may be amoebocytes or special nurse cells (*trophocytes*). The oogonium gives rise to an oocyte. When full grown, the oocyte undergoes the usual two maturation divisions to form the *ovum* which lies in the wall of a radial canal, ready to be fertilized by a sperm from another sponge.

FERTILIZATION

Fertilization is internal. When the sperms mature, the spermatocysts rupture, discharging the sperms into the radial canals. From here, they are carried by the outgoing current of water to the exterior through the osculum. With the incoming water current,the sperms enter another sponge through the dermal ostia and reach the radial canals. Here, each sperm enters a wandering amoebocyte or a choanocyte. The invaded choanocyte loses

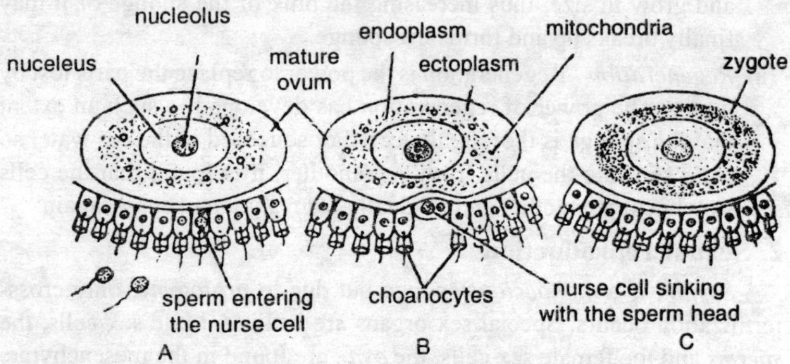

Fig. 3.12. Stages in fertilization *in situ* in a calcareous sponge.

the flagellum, withdraws the collar, becomes amoeboid and migrates into the mesenchyme. The amoebocytes and choanocytes penetrated by the sperms are known as the *sperm-transit cells*, as they serve to carry the sperms to the ova through the mesenchyme. A sperm-transit cell adheres to a nearby ovum, which forms a conical depression to receive it. The sperm loses its tail and its head swells up. The swollen head gets surrounded by a capsule. The capsule with the sperm head enters the ovum. This completes the act of fertilization and results in the formation of a *zygote*. The sperm transit cell now departs. The zygote gets enclosed in a *brood capsule* formed by lining up of the neighbouring amoebocytes. Early development of the zygote occurs within the brood capsule of the parent.

DEVELOPMENT

The development of *Sycon* includes the early embryonic period and larval period followed by metamorphosis.

I. Embryonic period

(a) Cleavage. The fertilized egg undergoes maturation and starts development within the mesenchyme of the parent. It undergoes equal and *holoblastic cleavage.* The first three cleavages are verticle forming 8 blastomeres. The horizontal division then divides the blastomeres unequally and 16 blastomeres produced, 8 are large cells or *marcromeres* lying next to the parent choanoderm. They are destigned to form future epidermis. Eight smaller cells or *micromeres* give rise to future choanocytes. At this stage, the embryo lies just beneath the maternal choanocyte layer as a flattened disc-shaped body. The micromeres undergo rapid mitosis to form several micromeres, elongate and each develops a flagellum on its inner end facing the blastocoel. The macromeres do not divide for sometime, become rounded and granular and an opening is formed in their middle which helps in the ingestion of adjacent maternal cells. This stage may be called as *blastula* with a blastocoel between both the tiers.

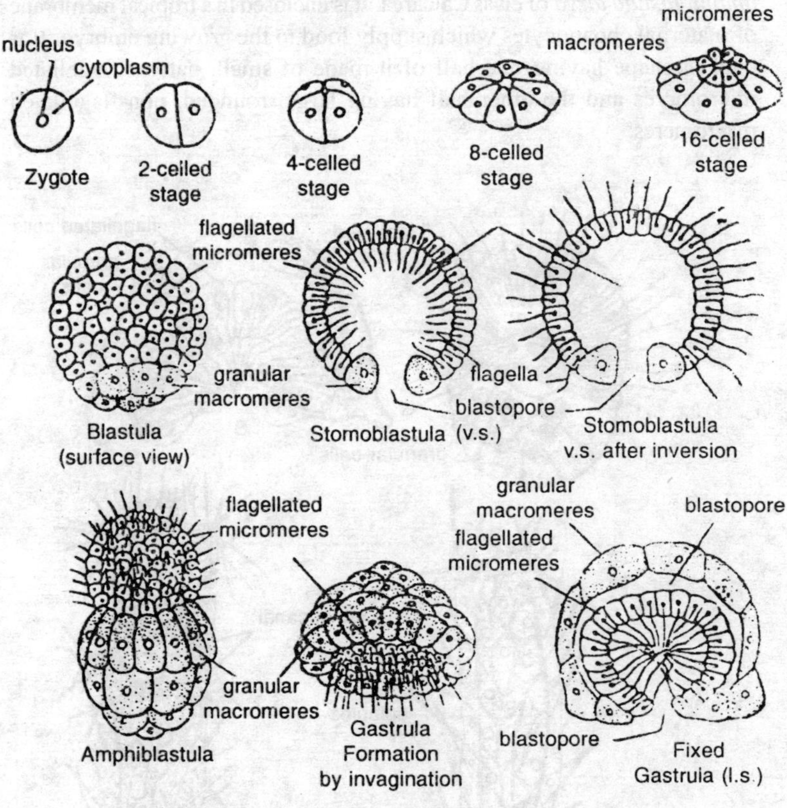

Fig. 3.13. Development of *Scypha*.

(b) Stomoblastula. In the stomoblastula, its one side is composed of many small elongated and flagellated *micromeres* and the other side is composed for eight rounded cells called *macromeres*. The blastocoel communicates to outside through an opening, the *mouth*, between the macromeres. This mouth is used for engulfing the surrounding amoebocytes for nutrition.

(c) Amphiblastula. The columnar flagellated cells of the stomoblastula continue to multiply. As a result of the pressure exercised, the entire embryo turns inside out by the mouth so that the flagella now point outwards.

After this inversion, the macromeres, also multiply and as they progress on all sides, the mouth of the larva is closed. As a result of further multiplication of cells, the larva becomes slightly elongated. A pigment and an eye spot develop at the anterior pole. This is the typical flagellated *amphiblastula larva* of class Calcarea. It is enclosed in a tropical membrane of maternal choanocytes which supply food to the growing embryo. It is oval in shape having one half of it made of small, narrow flagellated micromeres and the other half having large, rounded, non-flagellated macromeres.

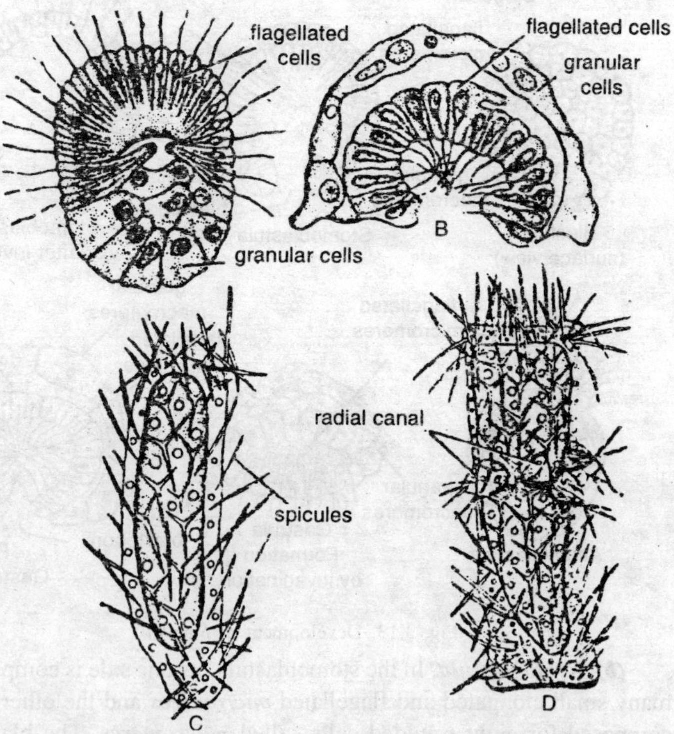

Fig. 3.14. Later stages of development of *Scypha*.

(d) Gastrula. Ultimately the amphiblastula settles down and undergoes gastrualtion. The macromeres multiply more rapidly than the micromeres, so that the flagellated half of the larva is invaginated into and overgrown by the granular non-flagellated half. The larva now becomes a typical double-walled *gastrula* with a *blastopore* at the invaginated side.

METAMORPHOSIS

After swimming for sometime, the flagellated half of the larva invaginates into or is overgrown by the large non-flagellated cells. With this process, the single-layered amphiblastula larva changes into a two layered *gastrula* with an opening, the *blastopore*, at the invaginated end. Outer layer of the gastrula consists of the non-flagellated granular cells and the inner of the flagellated cells. Gastrulation, thus, in a way reverses the inversion that took place at the stomoblastula stage.

The gastrula soon fixes itself to some substratum by its blastoporal end and grows into a cylindrical structure. Its blastopore closes by the growth of both the layers of cells along the substratum. At its free end develops a perforation which becomes the osculum. The outer non-flagellated cells flatten to form the dermal layer of pinacocytes. The inner flagellated cells for a time line the entire cavity which is the future spongocoel. Pores appear in the sides of the cylinder and start functioning as the dermal ostia. Through them water enters the spongocoel and leaves it through the osculum. At this stage the young sponge resembles just asconoid sponge *Leucosolenia*. This is known as the *olynthus stage*. The wall of the cylinder gradually thickned due to the formation of mesenchyme between the two layers of cells. Evagination from the spongocoel gives rise to the radial canals and invaginations of the dermal layer form the incurrent canals. The radial canals alone retain the flagellated cells, which by now become the choanocytes. In the mean time, spicules and various types of amoebocytes are differentiated in the mesenchyme. The scleroblasts and myocytes are derived from the non-flagellated layer, while the archaeocytes and other amoebocytes develop from the flagellated layer of the larva. The mesenchyme cells are, thus, differentiated from both the germ layers. With all this, a young *Scypha* comes into being.

Revision Questions

1. Give an account of the structure and functions of various types of cells found in *Sycon*.
2. What is canal system? Describe the canal system of *Sycon*.
3. Describe different types of spicules found in *Sycon*, and discuss its asexual reproduction.

4. Describe feeding mechanism and mode of nutrition in *Sycon*.
5. Give an illustrated account of the sexual reproduction and development of *Sycon*.
6. Give a net labelled diagram of the longitudinal section of *Sycon*. Describe the structure and functions of different types of cells.
7. Write short notes : (a) Porocytes, (b) Scleroblasts, (c) Gemmule, (d) Archaeocytes, (e) Olynthus stage.

4

Origin of Porifera

The evolutionary origin of sponges poses a number of intersting problems. The absence of organs and the low level of cellular differentiation and interdependence in sponges certainly seem to be primitive characteristics. But a specialized body strucutre built around a water canal system and lacking distint anterior and posterior end is found in no other groups of animals. Moreover, the cellular differentiation is unlike that of other metazoans. All these features suggest that sponges are phylogenetically remote from other metazoans. There are several hypothesis to show the origin of sponges.

1. According to the ancient view, the sponges originated from sluggish gastrula-like ancestors. But this primitive view is not accepted at ali.

2. According to another view the sponges originated from choanoflagellate protozoan. This theory suggested the possible origin from the colonial Protozoa, *Proterospongia*. It was considered in the line of evolution from Protozoa onwards to sponges. The followings are the resemblances between two :

(i) Morphologically dinstinct cells.
(ii) Presence of choanocytes or collar cells.
(iii) Presence of amoeboid cells in jelly-like mesogloea.

There are certain objections to this view as :

(i) The position of choanocytes is internal in sponges whereas it is external in *Proterospongia.*
(ii) The canal system is altogether absent in *Proterospongia,* even there is no any sign. It is characteristic of sponges.

The above objections can be ruled out due to the fact :

(i) The position of choanocytes in sponges is due to migration at a later stage of development.
(ii) The absence of alimentary canal gave rise to the evolution of elaborate canal system in sponges.

(iii) Development of spicules took place during their further evolution.

3. Due to absence of choanocytes in sponge larva a third theory have been proposed. This theory believed that the origin of sponges is from flagellate protozoan. This formed the colony and gave rise to early sponges.

Modern worker are of the opinion that sponges are lower Metazoa but they do not stand in the direct line of metazoan evolution. The following characters support this view :

(i) Absence of cellular layers in sponges.

(ii) Absence of division of labour as is found in Metazoa.

(iii) Absence of organisation like tissue systems (connective or nerovous) and organ systems (digestive system, reproductive system etc.)

(iv) There is no distinct division of somatic and germinal part of the body to carry on distinct physiological functions.

(v) During development in Metazoa, a gastrula stage arises when the future germ layers are established which later on differentiate into definite tissues or systems. These are never *reversed* during later stage of development but in sponges reversal of germ layers takes place.

The above facts are enough to separate them from direct line of metazoan evolution. But at the same time there are some distinctive features in sponges which should be taken into account. These important characteristics are :

(i) In sponges although there is no tissue or organs system each cells is independent.

(ii) The large terminal opeing *osculum* can be compared with *mouth* but they are not homologous, on the contrary are analogous because their origin during development is from different sources.

(iii) Although spongocoel may correspond to coelenteron of cnidaria but the presence of water canals lined by flagellated cells are not found in any other group of animals.

(iv) Poorly developed mesenchyme which is contractile in osculum region only.

(v) The presence of peculiar *amoeboid cells* which can form other cell types.

For the above facts *Hyman* considered sponges in a separate line from the direct line of metazoan evolution and the word '*Parazoa*' was given for the inclusion of sponges. Parazoa is a separate division of Sub-kingdom Metazoa.

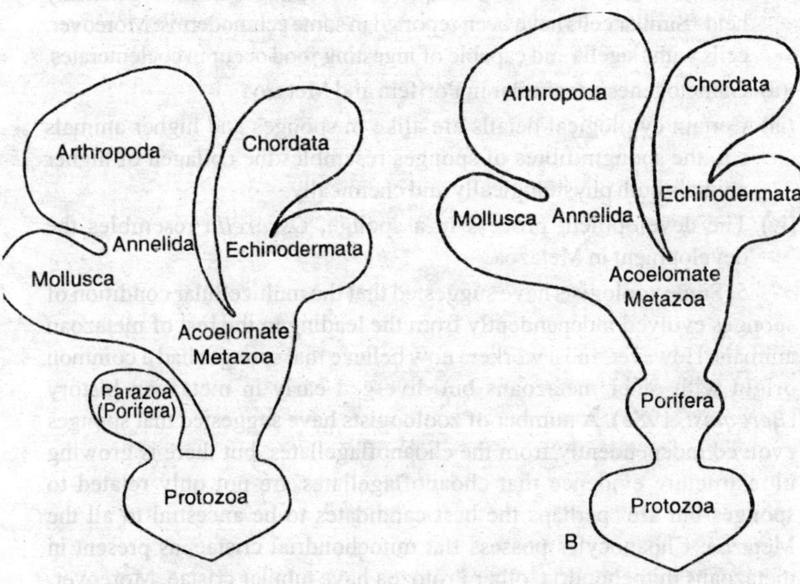

Fig. 4.1. Diagram of suggested phylogenetic position of the Porifera. A—Connectional view of sponges as an isolated subkingdom, the Parazoa. B—Tuzet's view of sponges in the mainstream of metazoan evolution.

4. *Tuzel's Theory. Tuzet* (1963) has suggested that the sponges gave rise to other metazoa through the coelenterates. This view seems to have some weight in it.

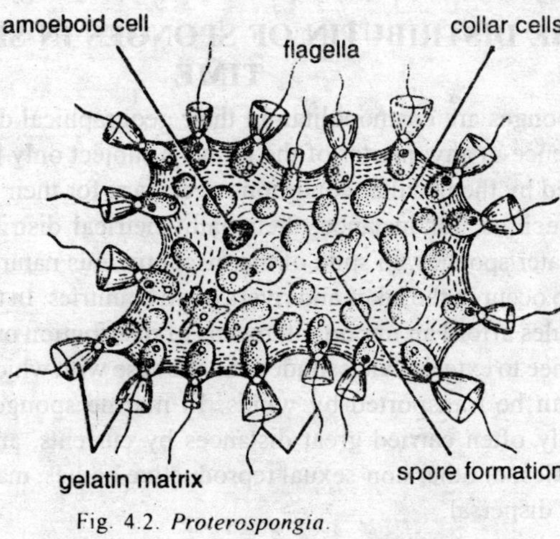

Fig. 4.2. *Proterospongia*.

(i) The choanocytes are not unique to the sponges as it is generally held. Similar cells have been reported in some echinoderms. Moreover, cells with flagella and capable of ingesting food occur in coelenterates.

(ii) Gametogenesis is similar in Porifera and Metazoa.

(iii) Certain cytological details are alike in sponges and higher animals e.g. the spongin fibres of sponges resembles the collagen of higher animals both physiologically and chemically.

(iv) The development process in a sponge, *Oscarella* resembles the development in Metazoa.

5. Some zoologists have suggested that the multicellular condition of sponges evolved independently from the leading to the rest of metazoan animals. However, most workers now believe that sponges had a common origin with other metazoans but diverged early in metazoan history (*Bergquist,* 1985). A number of zooloogists have suggested that sponges evolved independently from the choanoflagellates, but there is growing ultrastructure evidence that choanoflagellates are not only related to sponges but are perhaps the best candidates to be ancestral to all the Metazoa. Choanocytes possess flat mitochondrial cristae, as present in metazoans mitochondria, other Protozoa have tubular cristae. Moreover, the ultrastructural details of the flagellar kinetosomes and associated sturctures are essentially like those of metazoan cells (*Nielsen,* 1985).

Many of the specialized sponge features, such as canal system, certainly developed in conjuction with a sessile existence and the flagellated, exterior cells probably moved into the interior to become choanocytes. Such movement occurs in the embryology of living sponges.

THE DISTRIBUTIN OF SPONGES IN SPACE AND TIME

Sponges are cosmopolitan in their geographical distribution. Their occurrence in any quarter of the globe is subject only to the restrictions imposed by the peculiar conditions necessary for their existence in each case, such as, for instance, their bathymetrical distribution. Even the freshwater sponges, in spite of the discontinuous nature of their habitat, seem to occur in the lakes and rivers of all countries. In the latter case, the gemmules afford an important, means of distribution on account of their resistance to external vicissitudes and the ease with which, in many cases, they can be transported by winds. In marine sponges the larvae are probably often carried great distances by currents, and in some cases gemmules, or other non-sexual reproductive bodies, may also play a part in their dispersal.

Although no group or family of sponges appears to be limited entirely to any particular region, yet many are found more abundantly in certain regions of the globe than elsewhere, and may be said to characterise these areas. Thus in the Hexactinellids a far larger number of species are recorded from the Pacific than from the Atlantic or Indian Oceans; this is true both of Lyssacina and Dictyonina; but while in the case of the former the south temperate zone is the richest and the north temperate zone the poorest in species, the Dictyonina reach their richest development in the tropical zone. In the Demospongiae, the Keratosa, a group to which warm and shallow waters seem to be must congenial, are most abundant in southern and Antarctic regions. The Monaxonida, though a widely spread and very cosmopolitan group, are most abundant in the Indo-Australian region, a fact true especially of the very populous sub-families of the Chalininae and Ectyoninae. *Tedania* and its allies on the other hand, are more characteristic of the Patagonian region; while the higher systematic groups of sponges have the widest possible distribution, the range of individual species is often very restricted, though certain forms may be of widespread occurrence. Instances of the latter are seen in some generalised forms, such as *Halichondria panicea*, *Suberites carnosus*, and many others amongst Monaxonida. The species inhabiting deep water occur, as a rule, over wider areas than those restricted to the shore-line.

The classes of Porifera are better characterised by their bathymetrical distribution than by their geographical habitat. Speaking generally, it may be said that the Calcarea and Monaxonida are thore forms, inhabiting the higest littoral zone, and flourishing between tide marks; the Choristida, amongst Tetractinellids, and the Keratosa are most abundant just below tide marks, down to about 50 fathoms; the Lithistida characterise a slightly deeper belt, from 100 to 150 fathoms; while the Hexactinellids are typical inhabitants of deep wateer, the Dictyonina occurring in moderate depths, near the coast, and the Lyssacina in the abyssal regions far from the coast. In very case, however, the limits of these generalizations are overstepped by particular species. Thus *Thenea muricata* has been recorded from 1913 fathoms and may Monaxonia have speread down to great depths, as, for example, *Cludorhiza longipinna* from 3000 fathoms. It has already been pointed out as an interesting fact that the influence of an abyssal habitat upon these characteristic littoral forms, is to cause them to exchange their irregular body form for a symmetrical mode of growth, which is clearly secondary and newly acquired.

The geological record of the Porifera is largely dependent, as might have been expected, upon the nature of the skeleton. In each group we find those forms especially represented by fossils in which a rigid and coherent framework has been evolved; for instance, amongst Calcarea, the Pharetronidae; amongst Hexactinellids, those with a dictyonal framework; and amongst Demospongiae, the Lithistida. Since in each case these are the least primitive examples of the groups to which they belong, Palaeontology affords us but little help in unravelling the phylogenetic connections of the groups of Porifera. We know nothing of the past history or distribution of the more primitive groups, such as the Ascons or the Carnosa. The most ancient sponge known, however, namely, *Protospongia* from the Cambrian, is characterised by triaxon spicules of the most primitive and unmodified type, and the early Palaeozoic forms classed by *Hinde* as Octactinellida and Heteractinellida perhaps represent offshoots from a very early and primitive stock, which have not left descendants presisting to the present day. On the other hand, a remarkable feature of the forms mentioned is the relatively very large size of their spicules, which is probably not a primitive characteristic.

In general the Palaeontological record shows the extreme antiquity of the chief types of sponges, and their wide occurrence at all periods of the world's history, but is far from supplying links to connect the branches of the phylogenetic tree. We notice further that the forms most abundant as fossils are those which are now characteristic of deep water; but it is not necessarily to be inferred from this that the fossil forms were also inhabitants of the abyss.

Conclusion

Although the origin of sponges is uncertain, there can be little doubt that sponges diverged early from the main line of metazoan evolution and have given rise to no other members of the Animal Kingdom. A considerable number of facts would indicate that sponges are dead end phylum. Because of their isolated phylogentic position, the sponges have often been spearated from the other multicellular animals (Eumetazoa) and placed in a separate sub-kingdom, the *parazoa*.

5

Affinities and Position of Porifera

There has been controversy over the nature and affinities of the sponges ever since they were discovered. *Aristotle* (384-322 B.C.) was the first to recognize them as animals. Since his time, there has been difference of opinion about the nature of sponges. Some naturalists regarded them as plants, while others as animals and still many others considered them to be both plants and animals.

Once sponges were considered to be plants on the basis of following characters.

1. In structure, sponges are plant-like.
2. They are irregular and sometimes branched.
3. The colours are also quite different. Some are grey, others are red, yellow, blue etc.
4. Like aquatic plants, the sponges live attached to substratum.
5. They do not show any responce to the stimuli when touched.
6. Locomotion is absent.
7. They have power of regeneration.
8. Asexual reproduction by budding.

It was only 1857 that the sponges were fully recognized as animals. *Ellis* (1765) pointed out that the sponges showed sign of live by drawing in and expelling out a regular current of water. *Robert Grant* (1825) definitely proved that sponges were animals and not plats. He found water enters into body of a sponge by means of minute pores and passes out through osculm.

Following characteristics regard sponges as animal :

1. These are either radially symmeterical or asymmetrical.
2. Presence of many canals.
3. Unique type of skeleton in sponges, consisting of spicules and spongin fibers.

4. Digestion intracellular.
5. Multicellular animals without organs and systems.

Grant (1836) studies morphology and physiology of sponges and created the group *Porifera* for them. In 19th century, other names suggested by zoologists were : Spongiae, Spongida, Spongiaria etc.

Regarding the affinities of the sponges in the animal kingdom, there are two views.

1. Affinities with Protozoa.
2. Affinities with Metazoa.

1. Affinities with Protozoa

de Blainville (1816) separated sponges into a group, Spongiaria allied to Protozoa. *H.J. Clarke* (1866) first demonstrated the collar-cells and suggested that sponges are colonial Protozoa. The general affinities of sponges with the colonial Protozoa are due to *Proterospongia,* a member of the Protozoa.

The points of resemblance between the two groups are the following :

1. *Proterospongia* is a colony of collared Mastigophora placed in a mass of gelatinous matter having amoeboid zooids. These amoeboid zooids resemble to, and do the same functions as, amoeboid wandering cells of sponges.
2. It is natural that such an organism may develop into a sponge, thus, *Proterospongia* may be regarded as a connecting link.
3. Cells of the colonial *Proterospongia* resemble those of middle layers of sponges. There is a little *physiological divisons of labour*. Many cells of the sponges are also independent as individual Protozoa.

But this stage exists in some other members of Metazoa also and, therefore, *Parker* and *Haswell* regarded these differences being of degree and not of kind.

1. The development of the sponge is also fully worked out, which has no comparison with that of colonial Protozoa. The embryological investigations of *F.E. Schulze* have also belied the belief that sponges are colonial flagellated Protozoa.
2. Colonial Protozoa and sponges differ with each other as sponges posses canals, skeleton and somatic cells.
3. *Choanocytes* are internal in Porifera, while they are external in *Proterospongia*. However, some zoologists are of the opinion that choanocytes become internal only at a later stage of life-history.

Considering the above points of differences, zoologists have discarded the view that sponges are colonial Protozoa and that they originated from choanoflagellate Mastigophora.

2. Affinities with Metazoa

Linnaeus, Lamarck and *Cuvier* classified sponges as zoophytes allied to anthozoan coelentrates. Following are similarties between the Metazoa and Porifera :

1. Songes as well as coelenterates are both fixed and lead a fixed mode of life.
2. Both are diploblasitc. Well developed mesoderm is absent in both.
3. Coelom is absent.
4. The spongocoel of sponge opens to outside by osculum where as the central cavity or coelenteron opens to outside by mouth.
5. Same nucleic and amino acids are present.
6. Both can reproduce asexually by budding.
7. Gastrula shows radial symmetry.
8. *Parenchymula larva* of sponge resembles the *planula larva* of coelenterates.

But sponges differ from coelenterates and other metazoan in sevéral respects :

1. In sponges the cells are less specialized and interdependent than the metazoan cells. The cells are merely aggregation of cells which can assume various forms. These cells are generally found isolated in the jelly-like mesenchyma.
2. Tissue formation in sponges is restricted to the surface epithelial lining. The organs are absent as seen in higher metazoan.
3. Sponges are diploblastic where as metazoans are triploblastic. The mesenchyme and epidermis arise in sponges from the same embryonic cells so that their mesenchyme may be considered theoritically to be an ectomesoderm.
4. Osculum in sponges developmentally does not correspond with the mouth of coelenterates. The osculum serving as exhalent opening but in metazoan the mouth is inhalent opening.
5. Sponges do not posses stinging cells or nematoblasts like coelenterates.
6. Presence of inhalent ostia, inhalent canals, flagellated chambers are peculiar characters of sponges.

7. No distinct digestive system and mouth as present in many metazoan, digestion intracellular like Protozoa.
8. An anterior end is absent in sponges. The nervous system is absent to co-ordinate the various activities of sponge.
9. The development of sponges is most puzzling and difficult to interpret. In sponges during gastrulation the animal half invaginates but in Metazoa it is the vegetal half.

During larval metamorphosis the outer epithelial layer becomes the inner choanocyte layer whereas the inner cell layer becomes external to perform their function of epidermis and mesenchyme. This reversal of germ layers is unknown in Metazoa.

Position of Sponges in the Animal Kingdom

The most conflicting opinions have been, and still are, held upon this point. Up to the middle of the present century it was still disputed whether sponges were animals or plants. The discovery of cilia in them by *Dujardin* and *Dobie* was considered a decisive proof of their animal nauter, but their systematic position still remained a matter of controversy. By *Dujardin*, *Lieberkuhn*, *Carter*, *James-Clark*, and *Savile-Kent*, they were regarded as Protozoa, but with the progress of knowledge such a view has become incompatible with any rational definition that could be framed to separate the Protozoa from the higher animals. Mordern authors are divided, in the first place, as to whether the sponges are to be regarded as Enterozoa or as an independent phylum, distinct both from the Protozoa and from the Enterozoa (*Buttschli*, *Sollas*, and formerly *Delage*). Those who regard them as Enterozoa are further divided in opinion, especially as regards the homologies of the two primary germ layers. *Balfour*, whom at the present time *Maas* and *Delage* follow, considered them as composed of ectoderm and endoderm, homologous with the similarly named layers in Coelentera, but in sponges reversed in position at the metamorphosis; *Heider*, *Gotte*, and *Noldeke* also consider that sponges have nothing in common avove the gastrula stage, and the two latter believe that the sponge body is developed from the endoderm alone. On the other hand, *Leuckart* and *Haeckel* regard sponges as true Coelentera, composed of the same two primary germ layers, and built up on the same architectural plan; and *Schulze*, whom most authors follow, place the Porifera as a subdivision of the Coelentera, marked off by the possession of a distinct mesoderm, and the absence of nematocysts or tentacles from the remainder of the Coelentera or Cnidaria.

We have then three views to discuss, each of whic is based upon a distinct theory of sponge genealogy: first , that sponges are descended from a Protozoan ancestor distinct from that of other Metazoa; secondly, that they have a common ancestry with other Metazoa, as far as the diploblastic stage of development, and are therefore composed of the same two primary germ layers, but that after this stage they have proceeded along a distinct and independent line of evolution; and thirdly, that they have a common ancestry with the Coelentera, both being descended from a gastrula-like progenitor with a body wall composed of ectoderm externally and endoderm internally. The sponges would then be a modification of the Coelenterate ancestor in one direction, the Cnidaria in another.

In considering these views we may take the last first, as being the most easy to refute, although still that most generally adopted. The result of recent embryological work has been to completely undermine the Colenterate theory of sponge affinities, by demonstarting that at the metamorphosis the germinal layers become reversed in position, in a manner not suspected by those who first put forward this view. The Coelenterate theory assumes that sponges are composed developmentally of the same two germinal layers as the Coelentera, which also have the same architectural relations in the adult. The reversal of the layers makes it impossible, however, to extend the comparison to both the larvae and the adults. For if the comparison starts from the larvae , then the adult sponges are composed of endoderm externally and ectoderm internally. If, on the other hand, the adults are compared, and their constituent layers homologised, then the larvae of sponges are quite anomalous, consisting of an endoderm surrounding completely, or very largely, the ectoderm. Since the coelenterate theory has become quite untenable at the present day, at least in a strict phylogenetic sense, we have to choose between one of the two remaining views: either that sponges have a separate descent from the Protozoa, i..e. from the Choanoflagellata, an idea which has suggested the term Parazoa, applied to them by *Sollas*.

These were due to the following characteristics of sponges and considered the main features of *Parazoa* :

(i) Absence of definite tissues or tissue layers and naturally there is no organs or organ system. This is due to the loose assemblage of cells.

(ii) Absence of any kind of symmetry.

(iii) Absence of a true alimentary canal.

(iv) Inhalent pores are ostia and internal cavities are water canals.

(v) Special type of collared flagellated cells called choanocytes are present. Spicules act as skeletal structures.

(vi) Ingoing and outgoing water serves as nutrition, respiration and excretion; this also helps in reproductive activities like carrying sperms and in fertilization.

(vii) Sponges possess high power of regeneration.

(viii) Larval forms like parenchymula and amphiblastula are present in the life-cycle.

Now the situation as regards the systematic position is concerned is as follow. Sponges are on a side branch of the direct line of evolution. Although they have some superficial resemblances with Metazoa but show no embroylogical or genetic resemblances. Therefore, zoologists have separated them from Metazoa and have placed them in a separate sub-kingdom. They have divided the entire Animal Kingdom into three sub-kingdoms—*Protozoa, Parazoa* and *Metazoa* (or Eumetazoa). The sub-kingdom Parazoa includes the sponges. Again according to Tuzet's view sponges evolved from Protozoa and have been placed between Protozoa and Cnidaria in a separate phylum Porifera.

6

Histology of Sponges

In most of animals the body is composed of various tissues like epithelium, connective, muscular, nervous and skeletal. But in sponges there is cellular grade of organization means the body is composed of different types of cells lacking proper organization. The cells found in sponges do not organize into tissues. Sponges are *diploblastic* i.e composed of two layers-*ectoderm* or *dermal epithelium* and inner *endoderm*. In between these layers lies *mesenchyme*. The cells of these layers are simple and modified according to their function except one called *choanocytes*.

ECTODERM

These cells are generally called *dermal epithelium*. They form a covering of the outer body surface and the lining of incurrent canals. The following cells form this layer:

(i) Pinacocytes

These are large flat, closely cemented cells with thickened central bulge containing the nucleus. They appear continuous with adjacent cells. These are generally found to cover the outer body surface when they are called *dermal epithelium*. In syconoid sponge they also line the incurrent canals and spaces found inside the body. When line the paragastric cavity they are called *gastral epithelium*. These cells are highly contractile and thus can reduce the surface area.

In some sponges the epidermis is formed by epitheloid membrane which is a continuous membrane having numerous scattered nuclei.

Hexactinellid sponges have no definite epidermis.

(ii) Porocytes

In asconoid sponges (*Leucosolenia*) some of the pinacocytes are modified to form tubular cells, the *porocytes*, connecting the incurrent canals with the radial canals through their intracellular channels, The porocytes are thin-walled cells, open at both ends and with the nucleus present in the peripheral cytoplasm.. As has already been noted, the porocytes in the adult sponge are lacking altogether, Pinacocytes surrounding the osculum, outer or dermal ostia and inner ostia or apopyles are elongated and contractile and act as muscle cells, called the *myocytes*. They form the sphincters around them to regulate these openings.

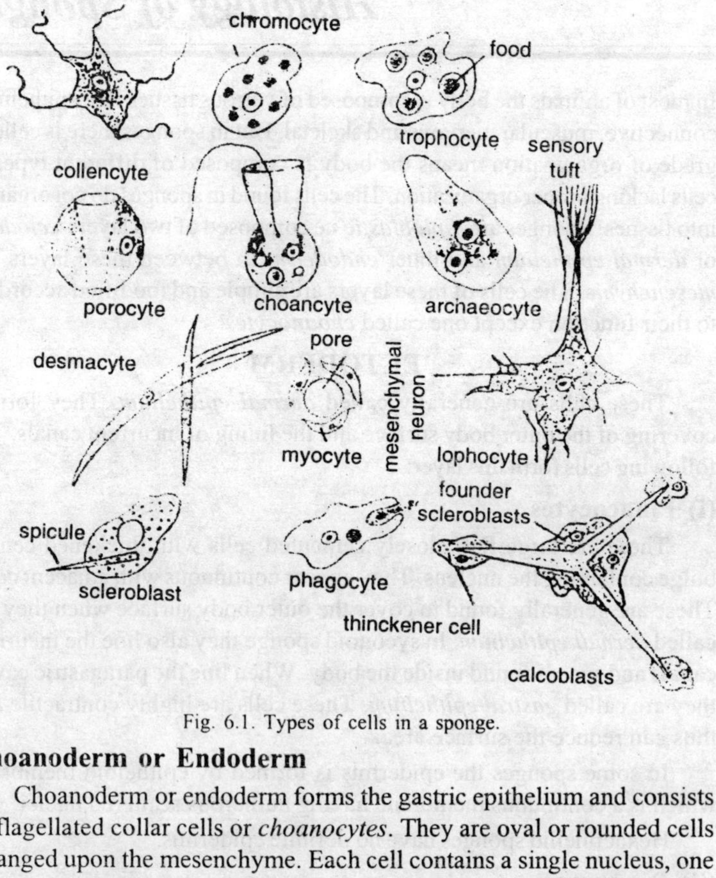

Fig. 6.1. Types of cells in a sponge.

Choanoderm or Endoderm

Choanoderm or endoderm forms the gastric epithelium and consists of flagellated collar cells or *choanocytes*. They are oval or rounded cells arranged upon the mesenchyme. Each cell contains a single nucleus, one or two contractile vacuoles, food vacuoles, reserve food, blepharoplast, rhizoplast and a single basal granule or kinetosome from which whip-like flagellum arises. The flagellum is surrounded at its base by a thin cytoplasmic collar. The flagellum has two central fibrils and nine double peripheral fibrils. The collar of the flagellum is contractile and is made up of a ring of erect and closely set microvilli which project from the cell. The choanocytes line the radial canals or flagellated chambers. The movement of their flagella causes a current of water.

Mesenchyme

The gelatinous, transparent matrix of mesenchyme is known as *mesohyl* in which are found special cells called *amoebocytes* which may be of the following types:

1. *Collencytes.* Star-shaped cells which are sometimes united to form a network.
2. *Chromocytes.* Pigmented cells with lobose pseudopodia. They probably import colour to the sponge.
3. *Thesocytes.* Cells with lobose pseudopodia and are laden with reserve food material.
4. *Scleroblasts.* These secrete the spicules. They may be *calcoblasts* (secreting calcareous spicules), *silicoblasts* (siliceous spicules), and *spongioblasts* (secreting spongin fibres).
5. *Trophocytes.* They are loaded partly or completely with digested food. They serve to transfer food from one place to another.
6. *Phagocytes.* These cells collect food from the choanocytes through their pseudopodia and also engulf excreta and damaged tissues.
7. *Archaeocytes.* Or *undifferentiated embryonic cells* that give rise to sex cells. They have blunt pseudopodia, large nuclei, conspicuous nucleolar and cytoplasmic inclusions. They may also be associated with transport of food and waters.
8. *Lophocytes.* These are amoeboid cells with a tuft of fibrils at one or both ends and occurs in connection with the pinacocyte epithelium. Its function is unknown but it may secrete fibrillar bundles.
9. *Desmocytes.* They are long slender cells lying at the basement of the canals.
10. *Gland cells.* They are derived from amoebocytes and secrete mucous.
11. *Germ cells.* Some of the amoebocytes (archaeocytes) differentiate into sex cells i.e. ova or sperms. However, in some sponges, they are said to be modified *choanocytes.*
12. *Myocytes.* These are elongated, narrow nucleated cells arranged around the apopyles, osculum, and ostia are also present a number of narrow elongated highly contractile cells, the *myocytes.*

    By their contractibility they can regulate the size of the openings.

The mesenchyme also contains the spicules which are monaxonic and triradiate in form. These serve to strengthen the body and hold it up right.

7

Canal System in Sponges

All the activities of their body of the sponges depend on the current of water entering through ostia and passing out through osculum or oscula. Inside the body, water current flows through system of spaces which collectively constitute the *canal system.* The entire physiological activities of the animal depend on the water current and the exchanges between the body and the exterior are maintained through the water current. The food and oxygen are brought through this current while excreta and reproductive bodies are excluded through this current. The perforations of the body of the sponge by a large number of ostia is characteristic of phylum *Porifera.*

All the living tissues of the sponges are soft and it is a direct need of the animal to maintain a constant shape with different canals or passage-

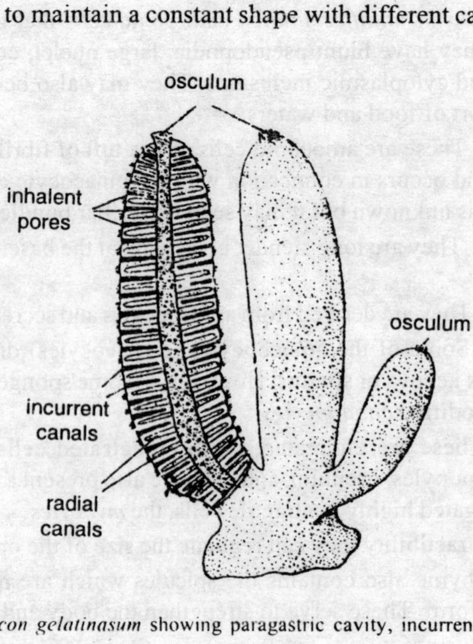

Fig. 7.1. *Sycon gelatinasum* showing paragastric cavity, incurrent and radial canal.

ways. Therefore, deeper layers of the body are provided with supporting *spicules.* Around the osculum, spicules are long and straight, while spicules situated around ostia are short and straight; around spongocoel they areT-shaped,while triradiate in the body-wall.

Thus, all the cavities of sponges with intricate passages of canals, traversed by currents of water entering by pores and passing out by osculum are collectively termed as a *canal system of sponges.*

A typical canal system is composed by following components :

(a) *Incurrent canal.* It opens externally to the outside by a small pore known as *incurrent pore* or *ostium,* but internally it ends blindly.

(b) *Radial canal or excurrent canal.* It is closed externally but opens internally by minute pores or *apopyles* into a central cavity or *cloacal cavity* or *gastral cavity* or *spongocoel,* which cannot be compared in any way with the stomach or intestine of other animals.

(c) *Prosopyle.* It is a smaller canal or passage-way connecting incurrent canal with radial canal.

The incurrent canals are lined by flat *squamous* cells and their functions are only to form water conduits and to form a smooth and firm surface.

The *radial canals* are lined by *collar cells* opening at the surface and are provided with flagella or whips. The lashing movements of flagellum procure the food particles and push them into the cell-mouth. Thus, this is food-capturing arrangement of sponges.

Spongocoel or cavity is lined by a thin gastric epithelium. It opens to the outside by an aperture, called *osculum.*

The arrangement, and complexity of the canal system varies considerably in different sponges and has been divided into four types :

1. Ascon type
2. Sycon type
3. Rhagon type
4. Leucon type

Ascon type

It is the simplest type of canal system in which the body is thin-walled, radially symmetrical and hollow due to the *central cavity.* This cavity is known as the *spongocoel* or *paragastric cavity* that opens to the outside by means of a circular aperture (known as osculum) at the free distal end of the cylinder. Numerous minute pores the ostia are also present in the thin wall of the cylinder. These minutes pores are regularly disposed intracellular apertures each of which is a canal like structure situated within a tubular *porocyte*. They extend from the outer surface of the body wall to the spongocoel. The water current reaches the spongocoel after passing through the ostia and goes out through the osculum. The body wall of ascon type of sponges is formed of two layers. The outer layer is called *ectoderm* and the inner layer is known as *endoderm*. The ectoderm is formed of thin and flat *pinacocytes*. The endoderm is formed by the *choanocytes* and lines the spongocoel. Between these two layers is a thin *mesenchyme* formed of non-living gelatinous substance. It contains different kinds of *amoebocytes* and *triradiate spicules* formed of calcium carbonate.

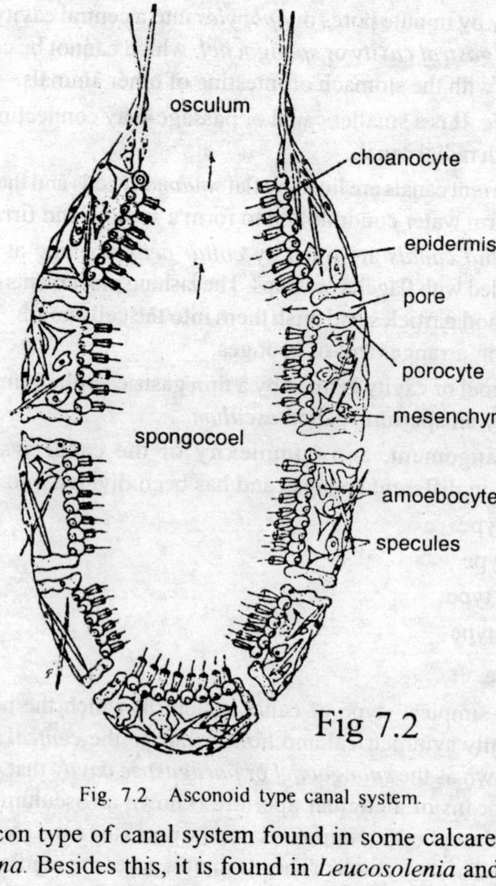

Fig 7.2

Fig. 7.2. Asconoid type canal system.

The ascon type of canal system found in some calcareous sponges like *Clathrina*. Besides this, it is found in *Leucosolenia* and some other simple sponges.

The course of the water current is as follows :

outside water→ ostium → prosopyle → paragastric cavity → osculum → outside.

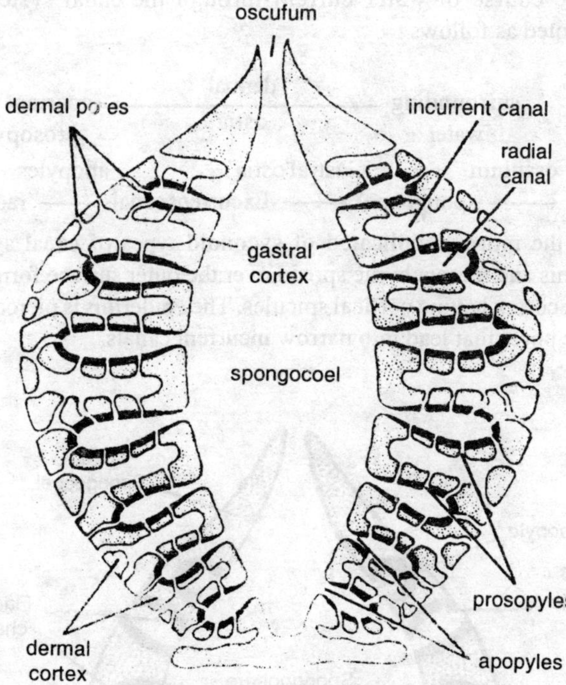

Fig. 7.3. Syconoid type of canal system.

Sycon type

It is more complex system as it is folded version of the asconoid body. It is found in *Scypha* and the embryonic development of *Scypha* clearly shows the asconoid type by the outpushings of the wall of an asconoid sponge at regular intervals into finger-like projections called *radial canals*. At first, these canals are in direct contact with the outside water but in most of the sponges, the wall of the radial canal fuse in such a manner that tubular *incurrent canals* are formed in between. These incurrent canals open to the exterior by dermal ostia or dermal pores. As these incurrent canals represent the outer-surface of asconoid type of surface, they are lined by *epidermis* while the radial canals which represent the outpushings of asconoid spongocoel are lined by *choanocytes*. The interior of the sponge in which radial canals open is a spaceous spongocoel which is lined by the flat epithelium derived from epidermis. The openings of the radial canals into spongocoel are termed *internal ostia.* The spongocoel opens to the exterior by a large single osculum. The wall between incurrent and radial canals is pierced by numerous minute pores called *prosopyles.*

The course of water current through the canal system can be represented as follows :

surrounding water —(dermal ostia)→ incurrent canals —(prosopyles)→ radial canals —(apopyles)→ Excurrent canals —(Gastral ostia)→ spongocoel —(osculum)→ outside

In the more complicated of syconoid types of canal system, the epidermis and mesenchyme spread over the outer surface forming a thin or thick cortex having cortical spicules. The epidermis is pierced by more definite pores that lead into narrow incurrent canals.

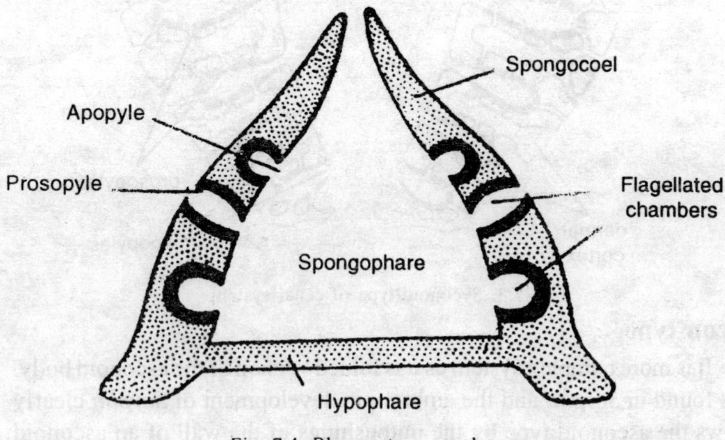

Fig. 7.4. Rhagon type canal system.

Rhagon type

This type of canal system is found in the larva of Demospongiae called *rhagon* which has a broad base and is conical in shape. Due to excessive growth of mesenchyme *sub-dermal spaces* are formed in its body wall.

The ostia open in these spaces which lead into incurrent canals. The incurrent canals open by prosopyles into flagellated canals which are lined with choanocytes. The flagellated canals open by apopyles into excurrent canals which lead into *paragastric cavity.* The paragastric cavity opens to the outside by the osculum which is present at the apex. The incurrent and excurrent canals may be complex and branched in it. The source of water through this system is as follows :

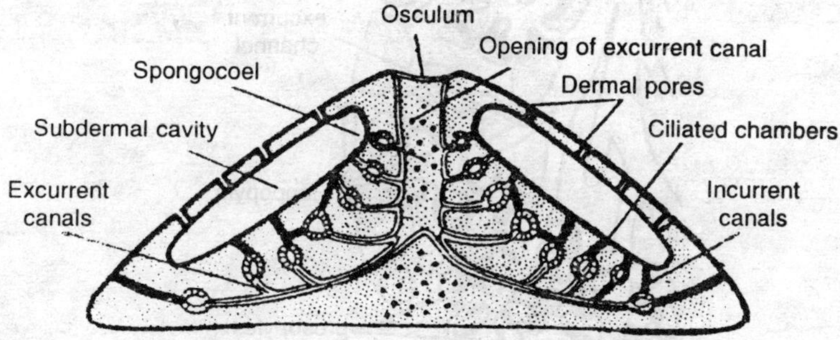

Fig. 7.5. Rhagon type in V.S. of spongilla.

outside water —ostium→ dermal space ⟶ incurrent canals —prosopyles→ flagellated canals

flagellated canals —apopyles→ excurrent canals —gastral ostia→ spongocoel —osculum→ (outside)

Leuconoid type

This type of canal system is formed from the rhagon type by the outfolding of the choanocyte layer. In this type, oval or rounded chambers lined by flagellated cells are formed by evagination of the radial canals. The surface is perforated by *dermal pores.* These pores lead into incurrent canals, which are found in mesenchyme. These canals are usually branched. In many cases, dermal pores open into subdermal spaces, which are large and provided with spicules. Incurrent canals open into small, rounded chambers provided with flagellated cells. The openings of the incurrent canals into the flagellated chambers are called *prosopyles.* The flagellated chambers open into the excurrent canals by small apertures, known as *apopyles.* These excurrent canals are united to form large tubes, which open into *spongocoel.* This cavity is largely obliterated. Spongocoel opens to the outside by the *osculum.* Leuconoid type of canal system can be divided into 3 sub-types :

(a) Euryphylous type

In this case the sponge has a flat broad base having an opening at the apex and looks like a pyramid. There are a number of flagellated

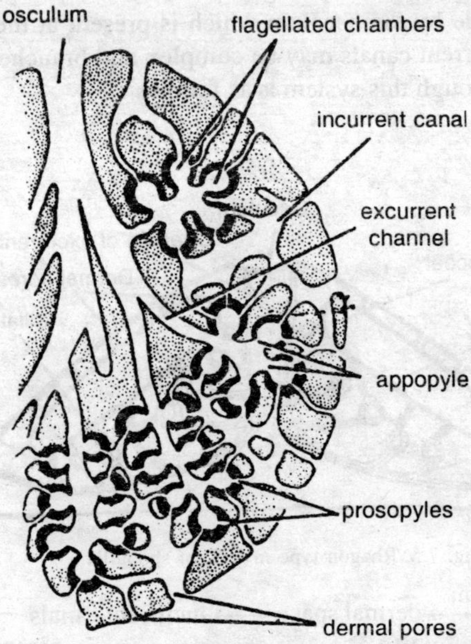

Fig. 7.6. Leuconoid type of canal system with eurypylous chambers.

chambers (*radial canals*) in the upper wall into which the prosopyles open. The lower basal wall is without flagellated chambers and is known as *hypophore* whereas the upper wall with flagellated chambers is called *spongophore*. The folded spongophore gives rise to incurrent canals.

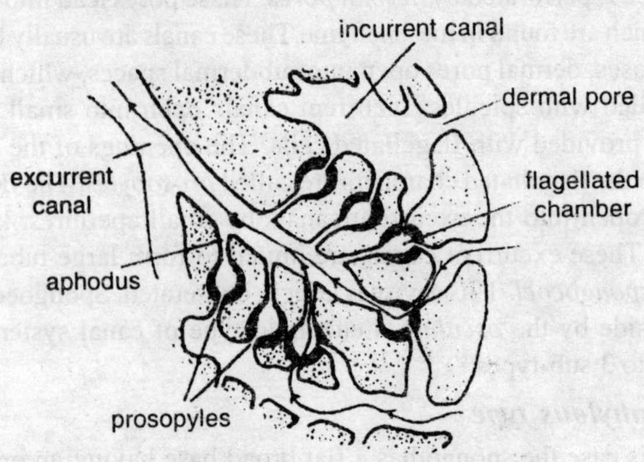

Fig. 7.7. Leuconoid type with aphodal chambers.

Due to this folding the flagellated chambers do not open into the gastral cavity but into the diverticula of it forming the excurrent canals.

(b) Aphodal type

In this type of canal system the flagellated chambers do not open into the excurrent canals directly but are removed from the excurrent canals by prolongations of apopyles into small canals called *aphodus* which are lined by the prolongation of the epithelium of excurrent canals into which they open. There is only one prosopyle to each chamber.

(c) Diplodal type

In this type incurrent canals do not open directly open into flagellated canals but open by narrow canals called *prosodus* which are prolongations of prosopyles. Thus each flagellated chamber has a *prosodus* leading to incurrent canals and an *aphodus* leading from it to excurrent canals.

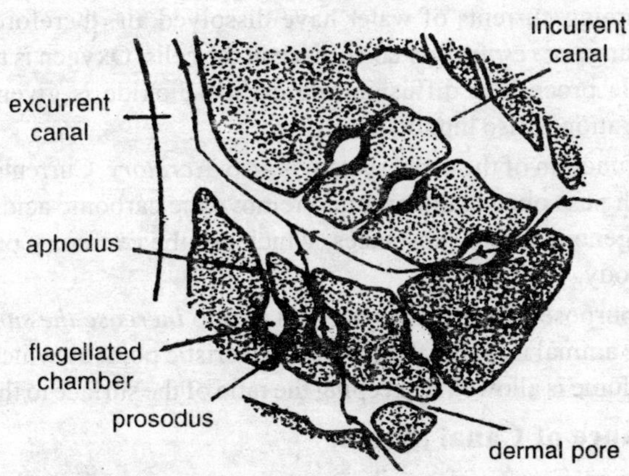

Fig. 7.8. Leuconoid type with diploidal chambers.

Mechanism of current production

To produce an incurrent or excurrent condition there are two factors which are essential :

(i) For entering water through ostia into the body there must be a pressure within it less than that in the incurrent canals.

(ii) For escaping water through osculum there must be a pressure within chambers higher than that in the excurrent canals.

But as the pressure in the incurrent and excurrent canals is the same, there must be a difference of pressure within the chamber itself and the lower pressure must be towards the periphery. Such a distribution of pressure is set up when each flagellum causes a flow of water towards the centre of the chamber.

Functions of the Canal System

1. The canal system serves the purpose of *nutrition.* It is regarded as a highway for the food through the body cells in the radial canal with flagella, which capture the food particles. Water-currents are produced by flagella, thus, waters flows into the central cavity or spongocoel. Smaller food-particles e.g., diatoms, protozoa and particles of organic debris are ingested into the cells protoplasm and digested. The digestion is *intracellular. Robert Grant* first of all observed the flow of water in the body-wall by adding powdered carmine to the water. Thus, canal system here does the same functions as circulatory system in higher animals.
2. In sponges, as a result of development of elaborate canal system, *massive growth* is found.
3. Streaming currents of water have dissolved air, therefore, gaseous exchange or *respiration* takes place in the cells. Oxygen is taken in by simple process of diffusion and carbon-dioxide is given out. The respiration is also intracellular.
4. The function of the canal system is also *excretory.* Currents of water, which pass outside the osculum remove the carbonic acid and other nitrogenous waste substances, which are the excretory products of the body.
5. The purpose of the canal system is also to *increase the surface area* of the animal in water. This is a characteristic point by which increase of volume is allowed by keeping the ratio of the surface to the volume.

Significance of Canal System

The significance of canal system in sponges is linked with their evolution from the simple to complex forms. This complexity was required to match with the increase in their body mass. Increased volume created excessive folding of the body wall along with breakup of incurrent, radial and excurrent canals into several interconnecting branches, creation of additional subdermal chambers and long tubular connections to reach the highly reduced spongocoel or excurrent spaces.

Revision Question

1. What is canal system ? Write an essay on canal system in Sponges.

2. Give an account of the main types of canal system in Porifera.
3. Give an account of canal system in various Sponges.
4. Give the structure and functions of canal system amongst Porifera.

8

Skeleton in Sponges

The skeleton of sponges is formed of spicules or spongin fibres or of both. The spicules are needle-like shiny structures. They have a *central axis* of organic substances around which inorganic substances are accumulated. An *organic sheath* is present outside this layer of inorganic substances. The organic substances of the spicules are in contact at places with the organic matter of the animal. The inorganic substance found in the spicules is either calcium carbonate or silica. The organic axis in silicious spicules is broad and distinct and is collected around the axis of mineral matter in the form of *concentric lamellae* which serially alternate with each other. In calcareous sponges the calcium carbonate is granular and the organic substances are absent in it.

The skeletal elements are typically quite separate one from another , but if united into a continuous framework, as is known to occur in at least one instance (*Petrostroma*), the union is brought about by fusion taking place between the spicules themselves, and not by means of spongin or any other form of special cementing substance. No distinction can be drawn in this group between *megascleres* (skeletal spicules) and *microscleres* (flesh spicules).

The calcareous spicules have a crystalline structure, and each spicule, whatever its form, behaves optically as a single crystal individual. Each spicule ray has an organic axial thread, and is enveloped in an organic sheath, easily seen when the spicule is dis solved by acid. The mineral substance composing the spicule is almost pure calcite, with traces of sodium, magnesium, and sulphates.

According to size the large spicules, constituting the main skeleton, are called *megascleres* and the smaller spicules which occur interstitially are called *microscleres.* Further, spicules may occur in several forms; they may be simple rod-like or may take the form of forks, anchors, shovels, stars, plumes etc. These forms depend upon the number of axes and rays present.

MEGASCLERES

They are larger spicules and named by adding *axon* in the number of their axes and *actine* or *actinal* in the number of their rays. They are of the following types :

A. Monaxon spicules

They are simple straight or curved rod-shaped or needle-like spicules which have only one axis. The growth of these spicules can be in one or both the directions of their axis. Thus they are of the following kinds:

(a) Monactinal monaxon

When the growth of the spicules take place at one of the axis, it is called *style*. Its round end is called *strongylote* and pointed end is known as *oxeote*.

(i) *Tylostyle.* Its round end is knob-like.

(ii) *Acanthostyle.* Many minute spines are found on its surface.

(b) Diactinal monaxon

When the growth occurs at both the ends of a monaxon spicule it is known as *diactinal monaxon* or simply as *diactine* or *rhabd.*

(i) *Oxeas.* Their both the ends are pointed.

(ii) *Tornotes.* Their ends are like spear-heads.

(iii) *Strongyles.* Their both the ends are round.

(iv) *Tylotes.* Their both the ends are like pin-heads.

B. Triaxon spicules

These are also called *hexactinal* and occur only in the Hexactinellida. Each consists of 3-axes crossing at right angles. Thus six rays appear which extend from a central point at right angles to each other. This can give many variations by loss or reduction of rays.

C. Tetraxon spicules

These are also called *tetractines* and *quadriradiates.* Each has typically 4 rays, not in the same plane. These may be :

(i) *Calthrops* : When 4 rays are more or less equal.

(ii) *Triaenes* : When 1 ray is elongated (rhabdome), bearing 3 smaller rays (cladome). If one smaller ray is lost it become diaene.

(iii) *Amphidisc* : When disc occur at both ends of a rhabdome.

A triradiate spicule is the most common spicule of calcareous sponges and results by the loss of the rhabdome of a traiene.

D. Polyaxon spicules

These spicules have several equal rays radiating from a central point.

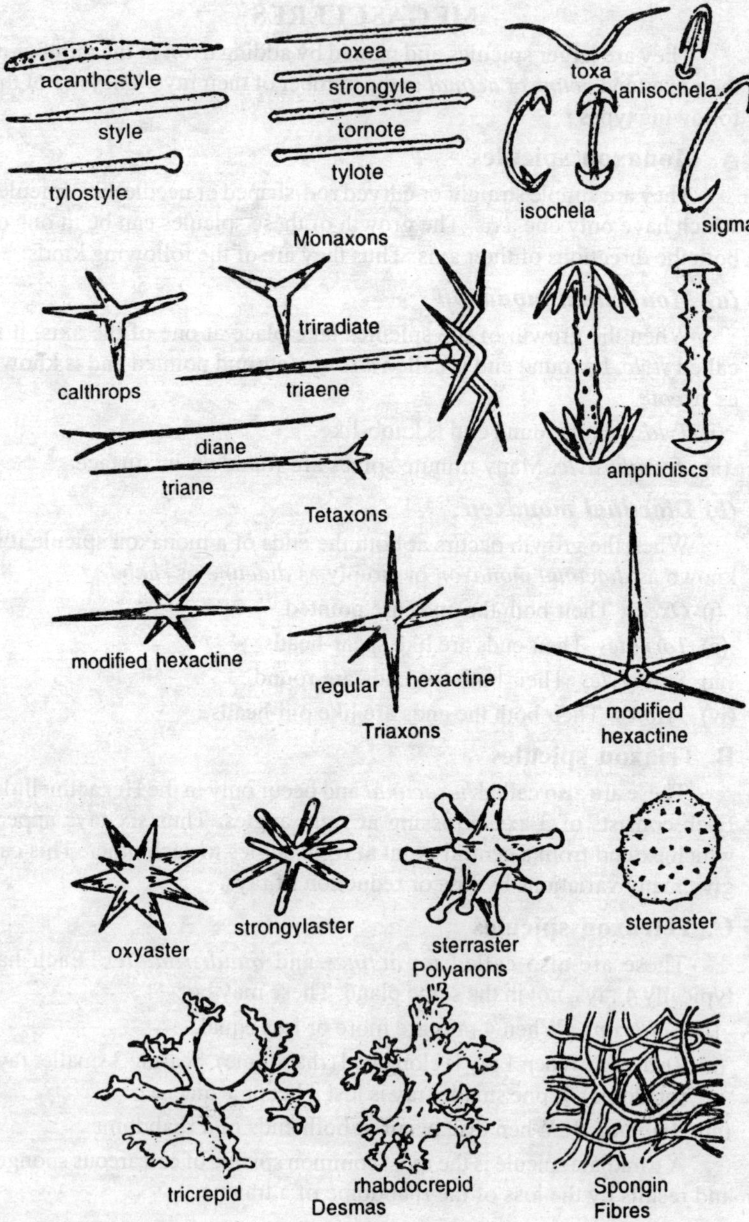

Fig. 8.1. Spicules and spongin fibres in Sponges.

E. Spheres

These are almost round spicules in which growth takes place around a centre.

F. Desma

Desma is a special kind of megasclere consisting of an ordinary minute monaxon, triradiate, spicule called *crepis* on which silica is irregularly deposited.

In the begining silica follows the crepis but later develops elaborate branches and when they are united into a network then it is called *lethistid.*

MICROSCLERES

The microscleres are minute flesh spicules which are scattered in the mesenchyme and sometimes are seen projecting in the canals. They are like megascleres in structure but small in size. They are of the following kinds:

1. Monaxon microscleres.
2. Polyaxon microscleres.

A. Monaxon microscleres

They are only diactinal and found in the form of straight or curved rods. The straight diactinal microscleres are called *Microrhabds*. They are of the following types:

(i) *Microxeas*. Their both the ends are pointed.

(ii) *Microstrongyles*. Their both the ends are round.

The curved diactinal microscleres or *spires* are of the following types:

(a) *Toxas*. They are bow-shaped.

(b) *Sigmas*. They are sigma-shaped.

(c) *Streptasters*. They are spiny spicules.

(d) *Chelas*. Curved hooks or plates are present at their both the ends.

(e) *Sigmaspires*. They are spirally coiled.

B. Polyaxon microscleres

Many rays radiate in all directions from a central point in these spicules. They are present in much large number than the polyaxon megascleres. Generally, they are called *asters*.

They are of the following types:

(a) Large centred forms

(i) *Spherasters*. The number of rays are definite in them.

(ii) *Sterasters*. Their rays are reduced and are seen only in the form of projections.

(b) Small-centered forms

(i) *Tylaster*. Knob-like structures are found at their ends.

(ii) *Strongylasters*. The ends of their axes are round.

(iii) *Oxyasters*. The ends of their axes are pointed.

ARRANGEMENT OF THE SPICULES IN THE SKELETON

The simplest types of skeleton are seen in the *Olynthus* stage, which furnisheds a natural and convenient starting-point for tracing the evolution of the skeleton. However complicated the structure of the adult sponges, in the *Olynthus* stage they differ from one another, as has been said, by characters merely of specific value, the arrangement and relations of the spicules being of a uniform character.

In the *Olynthus* the spicules from a single layer supporting and protecting the thin body wall. The monaxons are placed more or less tangentially with one end embedded in the tissue, and the other extremity projecting freely on the exterior of the sponge; a situation which explains the difference between the two ends of these spicules. The triradiates, on the other hand, are completely embedded in the body wall, and are so placed that one ray of each triradiate points downwards, away from the osculum, while the other two slant obliquely upwards and outwards to the right and left. In this way an unpaired posterior ray is marked off from two paired lateral rays; but the distinction between them may be one which is only recognisable when the spicules are *in situ* in the sponge wall, or the spicule may, on the other hand, exhibit a structural differentiation of the rays, correlated with their position and function in the sponge.

From the skeleton of the *Olynthus* may be derived that of any adult calcareous sponge by aseries of adaptations to the structural requirements of the various parts added during grwoth.

In the Homocoela the skeleton retains in all parts of the body the primitive arrangement in a single layer, seen in the *Olynthus*, but exhibits marked differences in the two families of the sub-order.

The family Clathrinidae is characterised by equiangular triradiate systems, a type of spicule doubtless corrected with the reticular from and growth of the sponges themselves. Monaxons may be present and some of the triradiates may develop gastral rays, but in the more primitive forms the whole skeleton is made up of triradiates alone. The primitive orientation of the triradiates, found in the *Olynthus*, is only ratained, as a rule, in the region of the oscular tube, while in the tubar system generally the arrangement becomes confused so that posterior and lateral rays cannot be distinguished by their position. In some forms, however, characterised by a more erect growth, such as *C. blanca* and *C.lacunosa*, the posterior ray is in dicated by its greater size, so that the triradiates become sagittal, while remaining equiangular. In *C.lacunosa* this feture is carried to an extreme in the stalk, where a distinct peduncular skeleton is developed, composed partly of sagittal triradiate. Some species of *Clathrina* have triradiates of special from on the exterior of the body, as an instance of which may be mentioned the "tripods" of *C. cerebrum.* In forms with a distinct pseudoderm this membrane may be supported by a layer of special spicules forming a dermal crust.

In the Leucosoleniidae the triradiate systems, if symmetrical are always sagittal - that is to say, alate forms, with paired angles and well-marked posterior and lateral rays. Monaxons are always present in the species of this family. The sagittal form of the triradiates is correlated with the more erect growth of these forms, and the spicules in question have a constant orientation with regard to the canal system-that is to say, they tend to be so placed that the unpaired posterior ray points in the opposite direction to the course of the water-current. Hence in the oscular tubes the posterior rays point, as in the *Olynthus*, towards the base, while in the diverticula the triradiates become arranged with their posterior rays pointing towards the blind apex and the same arrangement is repeated in the secondary and tertiary diverticula formed by branching, so long as they do not exceed a certain length. In this way the diverticula, though arising as simple folds of the wall of the oscular tube or *Olynthus*, acquire a special skeleton of their own, distinct from that of the oscular tube in its arrangement, though not as regards the spicules composing it. When the diverticula have grown to a certain length, however, they give rise to new oscula which are formed by perforation of their blind extremities. When a new osculum is about to be formed, the arrangement of the triradiates which are formed at the growing extremity of the diverticulum first becomes confused, and then reversed, so that in the terminal portion the unpaired rays point away from the apex instead of towards it. In this way the arrangement proper to an oscular tube is acquired preciously, at a time when the physiological conditions that prevail are the exact opposite of those with which the arrangement of the spicules is usually correlated.

The arrangement of the spicules in the diverticula and oscular tubes of *Leucosolenia* foreshadows, and give a clue to, the plan of the skeleton in the Heterocoela. Taking the simpler syconoid type as the starting point for this group, we find that at their first origin the ciliated chambers or radial tubes arise as simple diverticula of the gastral cavity, differing only from those of *Leucosolenia* in that they are more numerous and retain a more simple unbranched condition, not giving rise to new oscula. Each radial tube has its wall supported by spicules forming a special tubar skeleton, distinct as a rule from the more internal gastral skeleton both in arrangement and composition, and representing, therefore, in the latter respect a slight advance in specialisation upon the state of things seen in *Leucosolenia.* In the more primitive types the organisation scarcely advances beyond this point, except for the formation round the osculum of a special peristomial skeleton, consisting for the most part of elongated monaxons, and of a peduncular skeleton in the stalk. But with fusion between the distal ends of the radial tubes, to form a context, a special skeleton becomes differentiated in this region also, so that the skeleton of the body wall in a typical sycon consists of three layers: (1) most externally a cortical skeleton, which is said to be "smooth", when it consists of triradiates only, and "hispid", when it contains monaxons, with or without triradiates; (2) a tubar skeleton composed of triradiate systems, some of which may develop a gastral ray, (3) most internally a gastral skeleton, composed mainly of quadriradiates.

The tubar skeleton shows two distinct types of organisation known respectively as the anticulated and the non-anticulated. In the former which is the more primitive, and directly comparable to the state of things in *Leucosolenia*, each radial tube has its wall supported by sagittal triradiate systems arranged in several series, each with the unpaired posterior rays pointing towards the distal extremity of the chamber. In the non-articulated type of tubar skeleton there is but a single series of these triradiates, each one situated near the base of the radial tube and sending a greatly elongated posterior ray towards the apex, which meets, and runs parallel to, a similarly hypertrophied lateral ray of a triradiate of the cortical skeleton. By interlocking of these two systems of modified spicule rays the chamber acquires a firm and rigid skeleton.

With the evolution of a leuconoid type of canal system the pronounced radial structure seen in the *Sycon* becomes lost and the elongated radial tubes become very much shortened and converted into the smaller spherical ciliated chambers of the third type of canal system. As a consequence the regular tubar skeleton disappears and is replaced by an irregular parenchymal skeleton supporting the chambersand canal system and making up the greater part of the thick body wall, between the cortical and gastral layers of the skeleton.

According to their position in the sponge body the spicules of Hexactinellids may be divided in several categories, corresponding to the regions of the body which it is their function to support or protect.

1. Prostalia

Defensive spicules, usually diactinal monaxons, which projec. over the surface of the body, only found in Lyssacina. A special differentiation of such spicules may form a protecting fringe round the osculum, or an anchoring root tuft at the base. Those scattered over the general surface of the body are termed pleuralia.

2. Dermalia

Spicules supporting the dermal membrane; usually hexactinal or pentactinal, with four similar rays lying embedded in the membrane. They are distinguished as autodermalia, or hypodermalia, according as their axial cross is placed within, or beneath, the dermal membrane.

3. Gastralia

Spicules similar in form and function to the last named, but supporting the gastral membrane.

4. Parenchymalia

Spicules supporting the general parenchyma and the chambers between the dermal and gastral membranes. In the most primitive types of skeleton, as seen in *Holascus* and *Farrea*, the parenchymal skeleton consists of large regular hexactines (principalia), aranged to correspond with the intervals between the thimble-shaped chambers, two rays being disposed radially and four tangentially. This primitive type of skeleton may become much modified in form, and supplemented by other spicules(comitalia). In the sub-order Dictyonina and in many Lyssacina the principal spicules of the parenchyma are united in to a continuous framework, and distrinuished as dictyonalia.

Union of the spicules

In many Hexactinellids the spicules remain spearate from one another and simply interlock. In other cases some of the spicules of the parenchyma become united to form a continuous framework. This union is always effected by secondary deposits of silica, never by spongin.

In the simplest method of union, characteristic of Dictyonina, two parallel rays become apposed and united by concentric layers of silica into a beam, in which the primitive component rays are distinguishable by their separate axial canals. In other cases the end of a ray of one spicule become soldered to the central node, at which the rays intersect, in another. In other cases again the rays of adjoining apicules crossed in any direction are bound together by web-like elevations grow out from the sides of opposite rays, meet, and finally fuse to form a connecting siliceous bridge or synapticula. Since all these secondary deposits of cementing siliceous material are without axial canals, they can easily be distinguished from the ture spicules.

In the Dictyonina the principal spicules of the parenchyma become united early into a framework, and are seperate only in the growing portions of the sponge. Their union imposes a check on the growth of the sponge in a lateral direction, but it can continue to grow in length or at the free margin; hence the occurrence in this group of tubular, plate-like or cup-shaped sponges, the former often very similar in form to those in the calcareous family Clathrinidae.

In the Lyssacina the spicules either remain separate (Hyalonematidae, Holascinae), in which case the sponge may attain to a huge size (*Poliopogon gigas*, and others), or they may become united into an irregular manner at a late stage in the life-history, setting a limit to further growth.

DEVELOPMENT OF SPICULES

The cells that secrete the spicules are known as *scleroblasts*. The spicule may be secreted by a single scleroblast or from more than one mother cell.

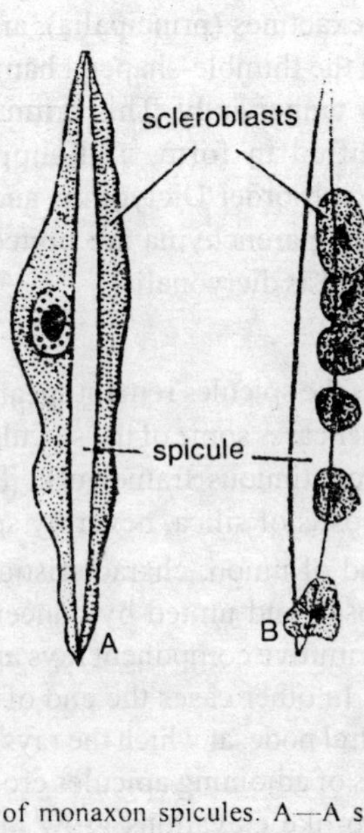

Fig. 8.2. Development of monaxon spicules. A—A single scleroblast of *Spongilla* secreting spicule, B—Several scleroblasts of *Leucosolenia* sccreting a giant monaxon spicule.

1. Monaxon spicules

In a binucleate scleroblast a small deposition of $CaCO_3$ appears. With development the two nuclei are separated wide apart and scleroblast divides into two cells. The cell lying towards inner side called *founder* gives shape and length to the spicule and the other cell lying outwards called *thickner* helps to thicken the spicule. When the spicule is fully formed both the cells migrate in the mesenchyma.

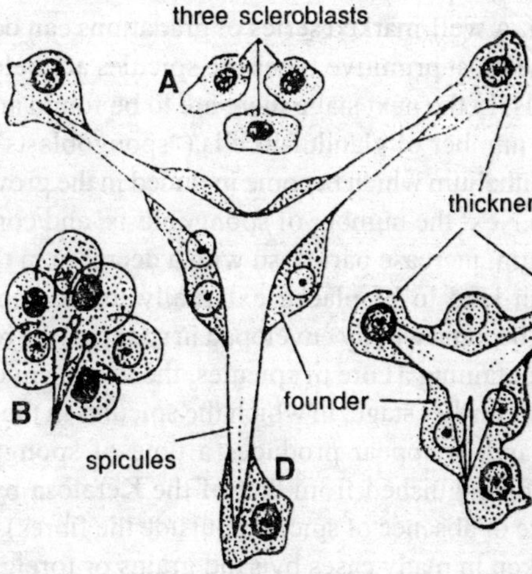

Fig. 8.3. Development of tri-radiate spicules.

In silicious sponges, the monaxon is of small size. Its complete development take place within a single *silicoblast.* According to *Maas* small monaxon spiculs of *Scypha* develop within a single scleroblast.

2. Triradiate spicules

To form a triradiate spicule 3-scleroblasts take part. Each divides and in each pair a small spicule is secreted. Ultimately these three spicules unite to form a triradiate spicule. Sutures may often be seen at the bases of the rays.

3. Development of quadriradiate spicules

These are derived from a triradiate spicule by the addition of fourth ray by an additional scleroblast.

4. Development of hexactinal spicules

A hexactinal spicule is secreted within a multinucleate syncytial mass, probably derived by repeated nuclear devision of an original silicoblast.

Union of the spicules and their Arrangement in the Fibres. Secondary siliceous deposits, for the purpose of uniting the spicules into a framework, are unknown in this group, thugh in the Spongillinae peculiar spicular systems of branching form, due to the fusion of several independent monaxons , are of common occurrence as an abnormor variation which may become so frequent that in some cases it must be considered as a normal feature of certain species.

Union between the spicules is effected either by means of fibrous tissue or by spongin. A well-marked series of gradations can be made out in this respect. In the most primitive types the spicules are held together, if at all, by fibre cells. In the next stage there are to be found amongst the fibre cells a certain number of glandular cells ("spongoblasts"), derived from the external epithelium which become included in the growing fibres and secrete spongin.Next the number of spongoblasts, and consequently the amount of spongin, increase paripassu with a decrease in the number of fibre cells, which tend to be placed externally to the spongoblasts. Finally, the spicules become wholly enveloped in spongin, the result being a fibre of spongin containing a core of spicules, the whole enveloped in a fibrous sheath. A still further stage, in which the spicules in the interior of the fibres atrophy and disappear produces a type of sponge skeleton which can only be distinguished from that of the Keratosa by arbitrary definitions (presence or absence of spicules outside the fibres). The place of the spicules is taken in many cases by sand grains or foreign particles of various kinds.

SPONGIN

Spongin is an organic, horny, elastic substance, resembling silk in chemical composition. Like nails, hair and feathers, it is a scleroprotein containing sulphur and chemically related to collagen, a horny protein. It is insoluble, chemically inert and resistent to protein-digesting enzymes.

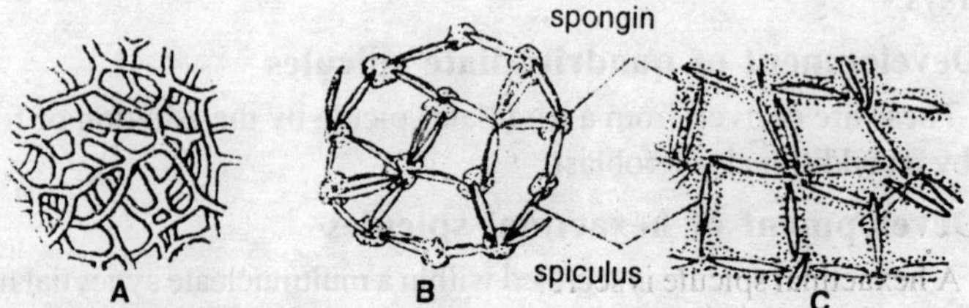

Fig. 8.4. Spongin fibres. B. and C. Spongin fibres with foregin particles and spicules.

Spongin contains a large amount of iodine reaching 8 to 14 percent in certain tropical species of the Spongiidae and Aplysinidae. It is interesting to know that old herb-doctors for centuries used bath-sponge as a cure for crop.

Two aberrant types of spongin skeleton have been described by *Haeckel* (1889). In his genus *Cerelasma*, placed by him amongst the Spongeliidae, the skeleton is described as consisting of thin spongin lamellae, which branch and anastomose to form a reticular framework. In the meshes of the skeleton are lodged numerous foreign bodies, each as a rule enveloped in a thin coating of spongin. In Haeckel's family stannomidae the skeleton is said to be composed of thin fibrillae of spongin, which may branch but do not anastomose, and between which numerous foreign bodies lie in the gelatinous ground substance. Grave doubts attach, however, to the nature both of *Cerelasma* and the *Stannomidae*, and it is very probable that they are not sponges at all.

There remain for mention, finally, the peculiar flaments found in certain genera (*Hircinia*, *Stelospongus*, etc.), combined with a spongin skeleton of the ordinary type. Each filament is a long slender twisted thread, slightly thicker in the middle than towards the extremities, and terminating at each end in a knob. The form has been aptly compared to that of an ordinary skipping-rope, with pear-shaped handles. Each filament has a thin sheath

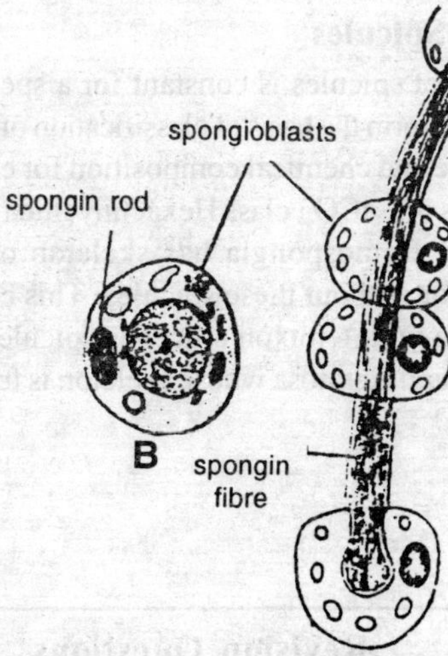

Fig. 8.5. Secretion of spongin fibres.

enclosing a softer medulla, traversed from end to end by an axial thread. The greatest uncertainty prevails as to the true nature of these structures. Their chemical nature has been shown to be different from that of spongin (*Schulze*); but while some authors are inclined to regard them as foreign to the sponge, and probably organisms of a symbiotic or parasitic nature, others consider them as true products of the sponge tissue. *Haeckel*, amongst the latter compares them with the fibrillae of Stannomidae, while *Fol* professes to trace their origin to fusiform cells of the connective tissue layer, and considers that the family Filiferae should be reinstated for the horny sponges characterised by the possession of filaments. *Loisel* suggests that they are intracellular spongin filaments of the same nature as the elastic fibrillae described by him in *Reniera*. The question cannot at present be decided.

Origin

The spongin fibres are the fine threads consisting of a soft granular axial core or medulla surrounded externally by concentric layers of spongin. The fibres are secreted by flask-shaped mesenchyme cells, called *spongioblast*, which are seen coating the fibres. The spongoiblast become arranged in rows and the spongin rod secreted by each fuses with those of neighbouring cells to form a long fibre. The spongioblast later become vacuolated and degenerate after having secreted a certain quantity of spongin.

Importance of Spicules

The structure of spicules is constant for a species so these are used in identification and form the basis of classification of the phylum depending upon their structure and chemical composition for example class Calcarea containing spicules of $CaCO_3$, class Hexactinyellida has six rayed siliceous spicules and class Demospongia has skeleton of spongin fibres and siliceons spicules or without these spicules. This class is further divided into Tetractinellida with tetraxon siliceons spicules, Monoaxonida with monaxon spicules and Keratosa whose skeleton is formed by only spongin fibres.

Revision Questions

1. Give an account of skeleton in Sponges.
2. Write an account of skeleton element in Porifera.

9

Physiology of Sponges

The physiology of a sponge is largely depend on the current of water flowing through the body. The water brings in the oxygen for respiration and food nutrition and removes carbon dioxide and waste products. Besides, the gametes (spermatozoa and ova) are moved in and out by the current of water. The volume of water pumped by a sponge is remarkable. A leuconoid sponge (*Leucandra*) 10 cm. in hight and 1 cm. in diameter has roughly 2,250,000 radial canals or flagellated chambers and pumps 22.5 liters of water in 24 hrs. through its body. The rate of water flow is fastest through the osculum and slowest through the flagellated chambers. For

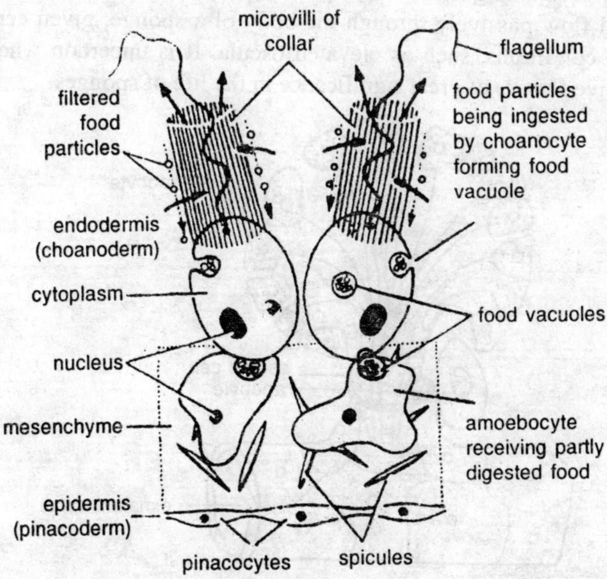

Fig. 9.1. *Scypha.* Feeding mechanism and digession of food.

these two regions have, respectively the smallest and largest total cross sectional area of the various passageways. Regulating the size of osculum controls the rate of flow, even stopping it altogether. In Demospongiae, control of the size of osculum is facilitated by *myocytes.* The myocytes are special type of underlying cells, which show some similarities to the involuntary or smooth muscle fibre in shape and contractility. The myocytes are located primarily around the osculum, where they are arranged like a band of circular muscle.

The water current is produced by the heating of flagella of collar cells or *choamocytes*. There is neither coordination nor synchrony of the choanocytes in a particular chamber. The choanocytes are turned toward the apropyle and each flagellum beats in a spiral manner from its base to the tip. As a result, water is sucked the flagellated chamber through the small prosopyles located between the bases of the choanocytes. It is then driven to the centre of the chamber and out the larger apopyle into the excurrent canal.

In many leuconoid sponges, the radial canal possess a *central cell,* which regulate water flow. By shifting position, the central cell can effect closure of the apropyle, and grooves on its surface can immoblize the flagella of surrounding choanocytes. When exposed to an external current, water will flow passively through the body of a sponge, given certain structural conditions, such as elevated oscula. It is uncertain whether such passive flow is of great significance in the life of sponges.

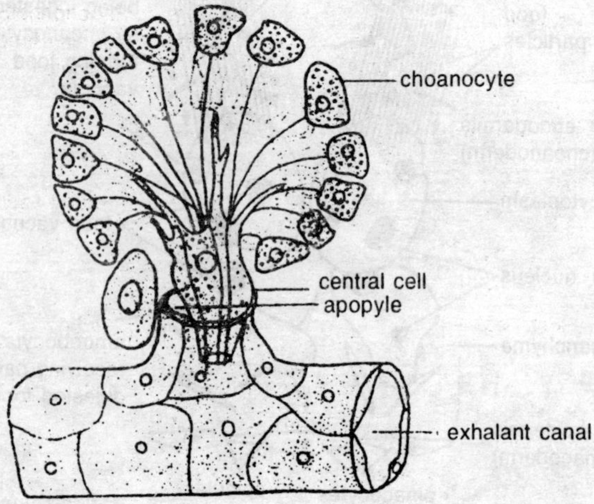

Fig. 9.2. Choanocyte chamber of *Suberites* containing a central cell to regulate the water flow.

Studies by *Reiswig* (1971) on tropical demospongie demonstrated that some exhibit a diurnal rhythm in the proportion of water current through their bodies, others exhibit an erratic endogenous water flow. External condition, such as turbulent water caused by stroms, may halt water flow regardless of internal conditions.

Sponges feed on extremely fine micorscopic particles. *Reiswig* (1971) studied on three species of sponges and demonstrated that 80% of filterable organic metter consumed by these sponges is of a size below that which can be resolved with ordinary microscope. The other 20% comprises of bacteria, dinoflagellates and other fine planktons.

In tropical waters, there is about seven times more carbon in the unresolved fraction than at the planktonic level. The ability of sponges to utilize this food source undoubtedly accounts for their long success as sessile animals.

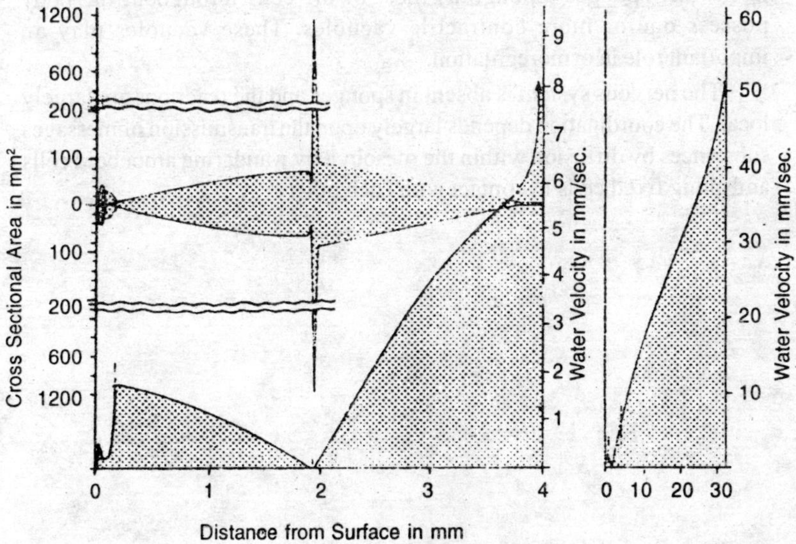

Fig. 9.3. Velocity of water passing through of different part of the sponge canal system. I-Inhalent surface, C-Choanocyte chamber, E- Apertures of exhalant canal, O-Osculum.

The food particles are apparently selected largely on the basis of size and are screened in the course of their passage into the flagellated chambers. Only particles smaller than a certain size can enter the dermal pores or pass through the prosopyles. Screening is also provided by protoplasmic strands stratched across the incurrent canals. Large particles of 5-50μ size are phagocytized by cells living the inhalant pathways. Particles of 1μ are removed and ingested by the choanocytes. Both chanocytes and amoebocytes can transfer their food particles to another cells called *trophocytes*. The trophocytes appear to be the principle sites of digestion. The food particles are digested within the food vacuole. The *thesocytes* act as storage centres for food reserves.

Adult sponges are incapable of any sort of locomotion. Some species can contract or alter the shape of body to certain extent.

There is no internal fluid compartment like blood or coelomic fluid as seen in other animals. The great volume of water passing through the canal system of sponge means the most cells are interacting directly with the external medium. Undigested food meterial and nitrogenous waste leave the body in the water current. The excretory waste is in the form of ammonia. Gas exchange occurs by simple diffusion between the flowing water and the cells in the sponge along the course of water flow. In freshwater sponges (*Spongilla*) most of the cells throughout the body possess one or more contractile vacuoles. These vacuoles play an important role in osmoregulation.

The nervous system is absent in sponges and the reactions are largely local. The coordination depends largely upon the transmission of messages substances by diffusion within the mesohyl, by wandering amoeboid cells and along fixed cells in contact with each other.

10

Reproduction in Sponges

Reproduction is the multiplication of the organism resulting the production of similar offsprings. Being sedentary, sponges multiply asexually as well as sexually. Asexual reproduction is more common than sexual reproduction. To tide-over the unfavoruable conditions some sponges develop capsulated bodies like *gemmules* and *reduction bodies*.

In sponges following types of reproduction occur :

A. ASEXUAL REPRODUCTION

It is a type of reproduction in which there is no direct involvement of reproductive organs. It takes place in the following ways :

1. Gemmation or Budding
2. Fission
3. Gemmulation
4. Reduction bodies
5. Regeneration

1. Gemmation or Budding

Exogenous buds are formed at the base of the branches. During bud formation, numerous archaeocytes collect at the surface and the pinacoderm bulges out to receive them. This bud gradually grows into

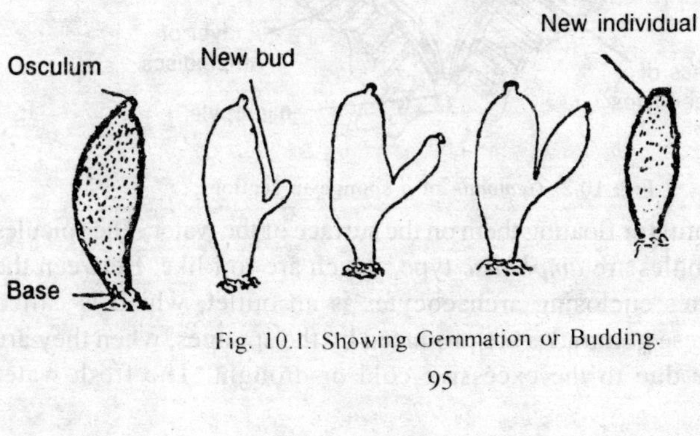

Fig. 10.1. Showing Gemmation or Budding.

adult and may remian attached with the parent but more commonly, the bud may constrict from the present and forms a new sponge e.g., *Donatia, Leucosolenia, Tethya* etc. In *Oscarella,* the buds are transparent and bladder-like. Due to light in weight they keep on floating and get dispersed.

2. By fission

In some sponges, multiplication takes place by fission, throwing off parts of the body. The sponge is hypertrophied over a limited area, developing a line of weakness. Along this weak line, splitting occurs and a part is separated from the main parental body which develops into a new individual. By budding this new individual takes the form of a colony.

3. Internal budding or Gemmulation

In all fresh-water sponges and in some marine forms, there is a peculiar mode of asexual reproduction, which takes place by the formation of asexual reproductive bodies or *gemmules.* Gemmule formation takes place by the gathering of *amoebocytes* probably the *archaeocytes* into a ball. This ball is surrounded by a chitinous shell supported or strengthened by spicules. Archaeocytes are filled with food reserves in the form of the oval bodies consisting of *glycoprotein* or *lipoprotein.*

Gemmules of *Spongilla* possess a peripheral layer having air cells,

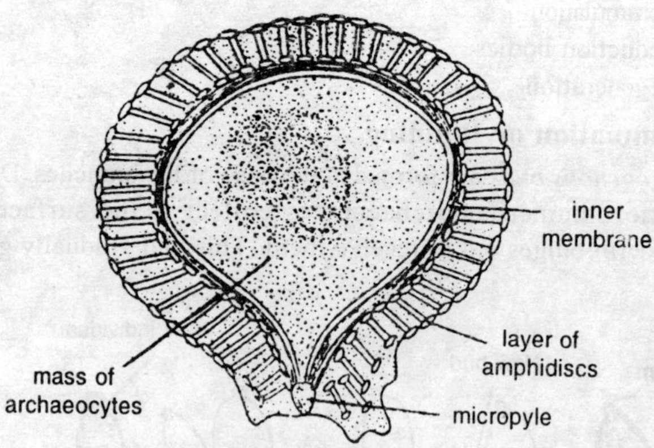

Fig. 10.2. *Gemmule* of a sponge in section.

which are helpful for floating them on the surface of the water. The spicules in these gemmules are *amphidisc* type, which are rod-like. Between the two membranes enclosing archaeocytes is an outlet, which is called *micropyle.* These gemmules are produced by the sponges, when they are unable to live due to the excessive cold or drought. The fresh water

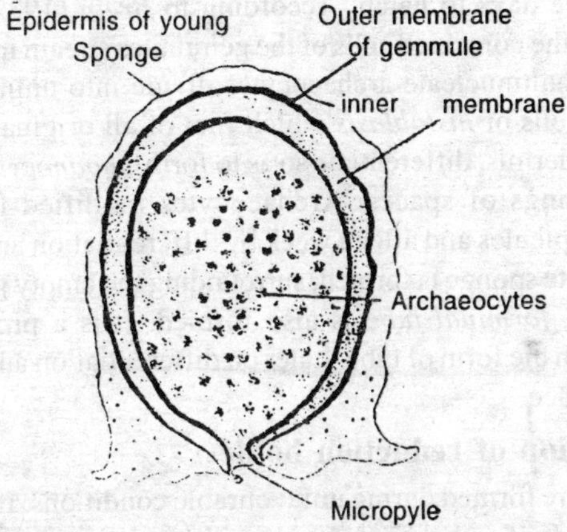

Fig. 10.3. Germinating gemmule of a sponge.

unable to live due to the excessive cold or drought. The fresh water sponges from a large number or gemmules in autumn and then disintegrate; gemmules are found in the remnants of the body of sponge or they fall to the bottom. Gemmules can withstand freezing and drying. They are, therefore, generally produced by the sponge in the autumn when adult sponges die. In India, gemmules are generally found on the approach of summer. On the return of favourable conditions in the spring, gemmules hatch. *Zeuthen* (1939) found that gemmules can hatch at any time at the

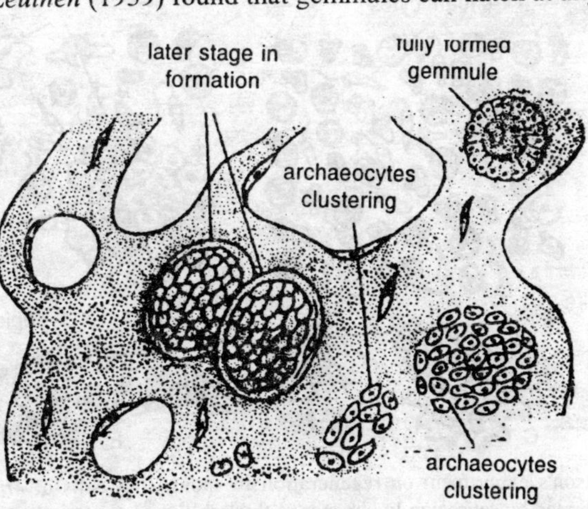

Fig. 10.4. Formation of gemmules in a marine sponge.

temperature of 21-33°C late forms hatch in two weeks, while in spring they require three days to hatch. According to *Brein* (1932) hatching takes place when the contained cells of the gemmules stream into the micropyle. The large multinucleate archaeocytes divide into uninucleate ones and into small cells or *histoblasts* which first of all originate and arrange to form an epidermis, differentiate so as to form *choanocytes, porocytes* and internal linings of spaces. Archaeocytes modified into *scleroblasts* producing spicules and after a week by differentiation and arrangement, a new complete sponge is formed, surrounding the empty gemmule shell. In some cases, *forminal tube* is also formed. It is a protrusion of outer membrane in the form of tube. Later on differentiation and arrangement of cells take place.

4. Formation of reduction bodies

These are formed during unfavourable conditions. It involves masses of many kinds of amoebocytes with epidermal covering that persists after the disintegration of the parent sponge. These reduction bodies can develop into sponges in favourable conditions. They differ from gemmules in not having an external layer of columnar cells with spicules.

5. Regeneration in sponges

All animals, particularly the less specialized ones, can replace their lost or injured parts. The process is known as *regeneration.* It is greater in

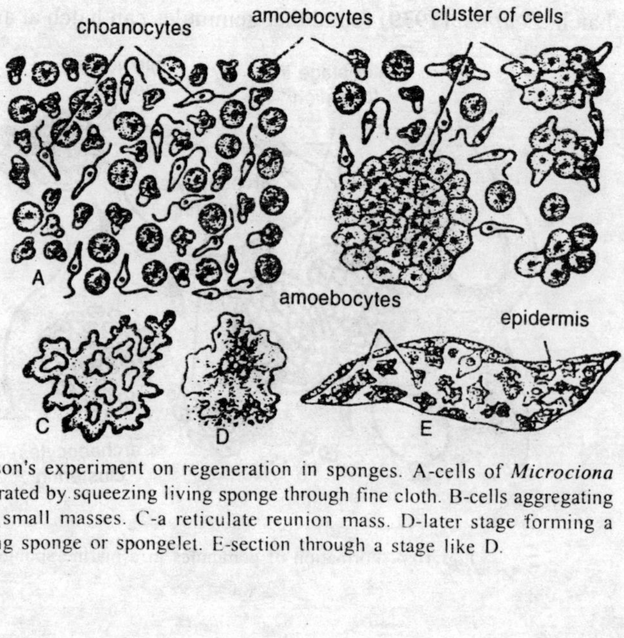

Fig. 10.5. Wilson's experiment on regeneration in sponges. A-cells of *Microciona* separated by squeezing living sponge through fine cloth. B-cells aggregating into small masses. C-a reticulate reunion mass. D-later stage forming a young sponge or spongelet. E-section through a stage like D.

simple animals and in simple tissues. Thus, epithelial tissues regenerate readily, whereas highly differentiated tissues, such as muscle or nerve tissues, have very limited power of regeneration. The sponges, correlated with their low grade of organization, have a high capacity to regenerate. If an individual is cut into pieces, each piece, however, small it may be, will grow into a complete or full-grown sponge. If conditions remain favourable. The regenerative power of certain sponges is quite noteworthy as demonstrated by *H.V. Wilson* (1907) by a simple experiment. If a sponge is chopped into small pieces, run through a meat grinder and then squeezed through fine silk bolting cloth, its cells are separated from one another. In a suitable medium, some of these disunited cells come together by amoeboid movements and unite to form small aggregates or *spongelets*. In course of several days these reunited masses aquire canals, flagellated chambers and skeleton, thus growing up into new sponges. Cells from different species of sponges may adhere temporarily but later separate, without re-forming a sponge.

B. SEXUAL REPRODUCTION

Sponges reproduce by sexual reproduction : by formation of ova and spermatozoa. Majority of sponges are hermaphrodite i.e., an individual possesses both male and female reproductive organs but some are dioecious (Gr. *di,* twice; *okies,* house) i.e., having the male and female reproductive organs in separate individuals. In bisexual or hermaphrodite or monoecious forms, germ-cells of the male mature earlier than those of the female, thus, producing sperms and ova at different periods. Eggs usually develop in the basal part of the sponge, while the sperms are formed on the apex.

Sexual reproduction in sponges, which live in shallow water, takes place at certain seasons of the year, whereas deep-sea sponges reproduce throughout the year. Sex-cells are produced from the archaeocytes but, according to some authors, sex cells originate from choanocytes. The ovum is formed by the enlargement of *amoebocyte* or *amoeboid* cells. It has a large nucleus and a distinct nucleolus. It grows and acquires food material. When full size is reached, oogonium or egg mother cell undergoes maturation divisions. In some sponges the sperm mother cell of spermatogonium is the enlarged amoebocyte covered by one or more flattened cover-cells, thus, forming spermatocyst. The spermatogonium which is in the spermatocyst, divides twice or thrice into spermatogonium, which produce sperms. Spherical bunches of minute spermatozoa are formed by repeated divisions. *Gatenby* described that the choanocytes dividing into spermatozoa. These spermatozoa have rounded heads and vibratile tails for rapid movement in water.

FERTILIZATION

Sperms of one sponge is carried by water current outside the body and enter into another sponge of the same species with incurrent water. This directly fuses with the ovum or get attached with a choanocyte lying near the ovum. The choanocyte with the sperm fuses with the ovum and set free the sperm which then fuses with it. Thus in sponge *cross-fertilization* occurs which is *internal*.

DEVELOPMENT

The fertilized ovum is called *zygote* which develops in the parental mesenchyme for sometime and gets covered by a capsule.

(i) Cleavage or segmentation

The division of zygote is *holoblastic* (*complete*) and equal or unequal. Ultimately there appears an embryo in which 8 cells are attached with parental tissue forming the future *pinacoderm* and the other 8 cells form the *choanoderm*. A cavity appears between these two and the embryo is now called *blastula* which leaves the parent body and grows into a free-swimming larva.

(ii) Larval forms

In all known cases, during development of embryo a free-swimming ciliated larva appears but the form assumed by the larva differs in different sponges.

In case of *Clathrina* and *Leucosolenia* oval blastula changes to *coeloblastula*. This has a single layer of cells, all alike in kind elongated, columnar and flagellated. At one pole is seen a pair of cells which are of a different character being large, rounded non-flagellated and granular which form *archaeocytes*. This changes into *stereogastrula larva* which is called *parenchymula larva*. The changes are :

(a) Some of the flagellated cells withdrawn their flagella and pass as amoeboid cells into the internal cavity.

(b) Archaeocytes also sink into the internal cavity.

(c) Soon these cells fill up the greater part of the internal cavity and the larva is now called *parenchymula larva*.

In this condition the larva attaches itself to the substratum and develops into adult form. Most of the *amoeboid* cells now migrate to the outside to form the dermal epithelium. The flagellated cells become internal and form the *choanocytes*. Ostia, osculum, spicules and spongocoel are formed and it attains this young stage.

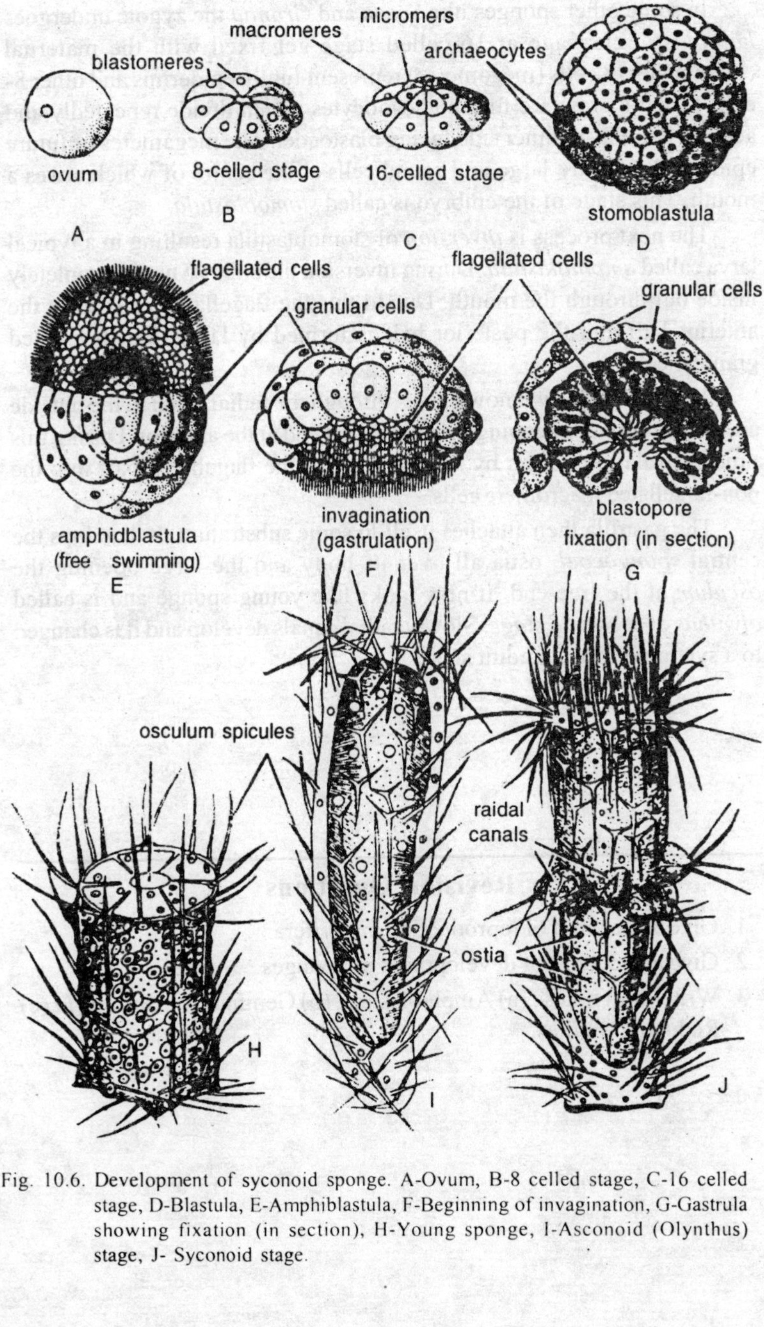

Fig. 10.6. Development of syconoid sponge. A-Ovum, B-8 celled stage, C-16 celled stage, D-Blastula, E-Amphiblastula, F-Beginning of invagination, G-Gastrula showing fixation (in section), H-Young sponge, I-Asconoid (Olynthus) stage, J- Syconoid stage.

In some other sponges like *Sycon* and *Grantia* the zygote undergoes *holoblastic* cleavage at 16-celled stage get fixed with the maternal choanocytes, 8 cells (megameres) represent future epidermis and other 8-cells (micromeres) are future choanocytes which divide repeatedly and acquire flagella on inner side facing blastocoel. The megameres or future epidermal cells are large and round cells at the centre of which arises a mouth. This stage of the embryo is called *stomoblastula*.

The next process is *inversion* of stomoblastula resulting in a typical larva called *amphiblastula*. During inversion the embryo turns completely inside out through the mouth. Due to this the flagellated cells form the anterior half and the posterior half is formed by large non-flagellated granular cells.

The *amphiblastula* now passes through the radial canal to the outside and swims forward keeping the flagellated end at the anterior. During this time gastrulation occurs by *invagination* of the flagellated part into the non-flagellated macromere cells.

The gastrula then attaches itself to some substratum. It develops the central *spongocoel*, ostia all over its body and the large opening the *osculum* at the free-end. It now looks like young sponge and is called *olynthus* or *asconoid stage*. Slowly radial canals develop and it is changed to a syconoid form or adult stage.

Revision Questions

1. Give an account of reproduction in Porifera.
2. Give an account of development in Sponges.
3. Write short notes : (a) Amphiblastula, (b) Gemmule of *Spongilla* (c) Reduction bodies.

11

Economic Importance of Sponges

Sponges are of great economic importance, they are useful as well as harmful to mankind.

1. Useful sponges to man

The flexible and highly absorbent spongin skeleton of marine sponge. *Euspongia* and *Hippospongia*, forms, after the removal of living parts, the bath sponge of commerce. The later is used for bathing, washing window panes and automobiles, mopping, ceramic work, and many more similar purposes. Today, cloth and artificial sponges of rubber or cellulose have greatly replaced the natural sponges for many purposes. Even then they are put to a wider variety of uses.

2. Sponges for Decoration and Presentation

Many people use certain glassy, transparent sponges (*Hyalonema*) for decoration purposes. Venus's-flower-basket is a beautiful sponge. It (*Euplectella*) is used for decoration and for presentation to newly wed couples symbolising a happy long married life like a pair of crustaceans which get enclosed within the body of this sponge for ever.

3. Sponges as Food

Although the sponges are not eaten by other animals like fishes etc. due to their disagreeable taste and unpleasant odour, but Nudibranch molluscs make a regular diet of sponges. Some parasitic crustaceans also feed on their tissues. Thus sponges have a food value to these animals.

4. Sponge fishing or sponge industry

Although synthetic sponges have become widely used, and largely replaced natural sponges yet natural sponges still have a great market, therefore, sponge industry is of great economic value. Since the days of Greece, the fibrous skeleton of bath sponge, *Euspongia* is used for washing and mopping. The water holding capacity of the skeleton is due to capillary forces in the fine spaces of irregular spongin network. The best and principle supplies of sponges occur on rocky bottoms in warm shallow waters of the Mediterranean sea and the Gulf of Mexico, Tarpon springs, Florida of United States the best commercial sponge fishing centre of U.S.A. where more than a million of dollars worth of sponges have been collected in a year. However, fungus infection reduce the total yield.

The commercial sponges are exclusively obtained from the seas. There are about 3000 species of sponges, only few have commercial importance. The zoological name, trade name and place of occurrence is given in the form of table below.

	Zoological name	*Trade name*	*Place of occurrence*
1.	*Euspongia zimoca*	Zimocca	Mediterranean
2.	*E.officinalis mollissima*	Turkey cap	Mediterranean
3.	*E.officinelis adriatice*	Turkey toilet	Adriatic sea
4.	*E.officinalis varlamella*	Elephant Ear	Turkey
5.	*Spongia graminea*	Grass	Cuba, Florida
6.	*S.barbara*	Yellow	Florida
7.	*S. dura*	Hard head	Bahamas
8.	*Hippospongia lachne*	Sheep's wool	Bhamas
9.	*H. grossypina*	Velvet	Bahamas
10.	*H.equina elastica*	Honey comb	Mediterranean
11.	*H.canalicula*	Glove	Florida

Sponges are collected by several methods, by drag hooks, by trawlers and by divers. In deeper waters, they are gathered by dredging or trawling or more commonly by divers, either with or without a diving suit known as skin divers. In shallow waters, sponges are gathered by the help of long handled hooks operated by the two men while one man rows, the other looks at the bottom of the ocean through a glass-bottomed bucket. The marketable variety is taken out with a two pronged hook, fastened to a long pole.

Sponges have great power of regeneration. The culture of sponges is economical. The large sized sponge is cut into small pieces and providing them the natural environment, each pices grows to commercial size. The best method of sponge culture is provided by Japanese. Two, important and largely used methods are given here.

The first method is known as *floating raft method.* A floating raft is prepared by tying several bamboos through sann hemp. The length of raft may be 5 meters or more. The raft is fixed to a place in the shallow sea by means of poles stuck in the bottom of sea. To maintain the fixed position of raft, metallic sinkers are used. Small pieces of sponges (about 8 cubic inches) are stung from the float with the help of thread. In due course of time large sized sponges are obtained.

The second method is known as *disc method.* It is somewhat difficult then the floating raft method. Central blocks of 5" × 5" × 2" are placed in sea water. These blocks are kept at a depth of 3-5 fathoms by means of floating raft made up of corked sealed bottles. The rafts are kept 2 fathoms below water level. The sponge pieces are tied around the metallic wires which stratches between the float and the disc. There should be a distance of 12 cm. between two pieces.

Both the methods are widely used in Japan. Out of all the cutting used as seed, nearly 50% are lost due to various reasons such as transportation, diseases, attack by parasites and enemies.

Living sponge is black in colour, smooth and slimy mass having a leathery covering. In the inside, it resembles to a piece of raw beef liver, both in consistency and colour. After cleaning so as to remove dirt, sponges are hung from the riggs of the boat and their protoplasm is allowed to decay. Later, they are well washed, beaten, bounded with a wooden mallet so as to break up any solid material such as invertebrate shells and ultimately by dried in sun, cleaned sponges are cut or trimmed, sometimes bleached, graded, sorted, and then auctioned. Sponges can be easily pressed for shipping due to their great elasticity.

5. Sponges and their association with other animals

Some sponges show commensalism as several crustaceans, worms, molluscs and fishes inhibit and live in the internal cavities of sponges for protection against enemies. They also get a good supply of food in the circulating water. The spongocoel of *Hyalonema* and *Euplactella* is occupied by a pair of shrimp of genus *Spongicola*. It is the example of commensalism. The shrimps enter the spongocoel in small and young condition as they grow inside their exit become impossible through the sieve plate covering the osculum.

Another example is that of a small family of crabs (*Hyas, Dromia* etc.) in sponges. The crabs cover themselves with the bits of sponges, algae, hydroids etc. with the help of a sticky secretion. The implanted sponge grow and moulds itself. This covering acts as caumoflage but also protects the crab from its predators.

Some animals pass their whole life in the dark interior of a sponge where they are well fed and developed their bodies are frequently modified to fit their tubular home. *Pearse* counted in one about 17,128 animals of 19 different species in a washtube sized sponge body.

Suberites, Ficlina etc. commonly grow on the shell of snail which is occupied by hermit crabs. The growing sponge completely surrounds and absorbs the shell expcept for shell opening. In the due course of time. The crab inhibits a spiral cavity in the sponge. The sponge conceles and protects the crab by its odour and disagreeable taste from the other animals like fishes and cephalopods. The crab takes the sponge from place to place into regions of fresh supplies of food and oxygen.

6. Harmful sponges

Sponges are not only useful to mankind but there are some sponges which are harmful to us. The boring sponge *Cliona* bore the shells of the oysters and barnacles and break them into pieces resulting their death. Some sponges produce poisonous secretions and when touched the skin is pricked by the poisonous spicules producing itching of the skin.

12

Metazoa

The highly plastic and successful protozoan organizational plan imposed but one serious limitation-that of size. An undivided mass of protoplasm becomes physiologically and structurally ineffective if too large. It suffers from lack of mechanical strength if flattened or elongated, and from lack of surface area if it approaches a spherical shape. Large animals are of necessity multicellular.

Metazoa have escaped being limited to cellular size through multicellularity, but some are smaller than the largest Protozoa. Protozoa form colonies, some of which have thousands of members, while some of the smallest Metazoa consist of less than a hundred cells, but among those few cells several types of non-reproductive cells are found. The main distinction between protozoan colonies and metazoans is somatic cell differentiation.

THE MAJOR TYPES OF METAZOA

The typical metazoan body is composed of layers of cells. The simplest arrangement is found in Mesozoa. The outer covering of these small, parasitic animals is formed of a single layer of cells, but no inner layer corresponding to an endoderm is present. In this they resemble a blastula. One or more reproductive cells occur within the covering layer which resemble some protozoan colonies. Their organizational level is above that of Protozoa, however, in the differentiation of the somatic cells of the covering layer.

Sponges belong to Parazoa. A single layer of cells forms the outer covering. Sponges have an internal cavity or system of canals-lined by a layer of cells, all or part of which are choanocytes, which resemble choanoflagellates. They ingest food and propel water through the canal system. Between the inner and outer layers is a mesogloea, containing a number of different cell types. Parazoa are separated from other Metazoa because the system of canals is not like a digestive tract, and the other organ systems found in Metazoa are lacking.

All of the remaining multicellular organisms are Eumetazoa. The body is covered by cells derived from the embryonic *ectoderm*. Typically, they have a digestive cavity, lined by cells derived from the embryonic *endoderm*, and a third layer of cells, the *mesoderm*, between the inner and outer layers. This layer is missing only in the hydrozoan coelenterates. The mesoderm is ultimately derived from either the outer or inner layer of cells during embryonic development, but establishes itself as a third embryonic layer.

GENERAL CHARACTERISTIC OF METAZOA

The general characteristcs of multicelllular animals have been mentioned, in part, in preceding. The critical characteristic is the presence of several types of somatic cells. Histogenesis, the embronic differentiation of specialized cell and tissue types, is therefore a characterisitc process. Although a commonwealth of cells, each meazoan functions as an integrated organism and the masses of cells are neither random nor chaotic. Polarity and the appearance of body axes are characteistic of Metazoa.

The metazoan begins as a unicellular zygote, structurally equivalent to a protozoan. It passes through a series of developmental stages in becoming a multicellular animal. Metazoan embryology involves an early, period of cleavage, dominated by a series of cell divisions. Cleavage is followed by periods of morphogenetic movements, involving changes in the form of masses or layers of cells as they are transformed into the various structures of the adult. The first morphogenetic movements result in the formation of embryonic cell layers, called *germ layers* . The layered origin of the adult may be almost completely hidden by profound changes in the germ layers during later development, or may be clearly visible in the adult, with the layers retaining something of their original embryonic relationships. The way germ layers form and the course of their development are of great importance in understanding invertebrate relationships. Histogenesis may start during early development, but the more detailed changes usually occur during later organogeny, after the organ rudiments have been shaped by morphogenetic movements. The morphogenetic movements produce certain body cavities during development. These cavities, and their relationship to the germ layers, are also important factors in recognising relationships.

CLEAVAGE-EMBRYONIC ORIGIN OF MULTICELLULARITY

Cleavage is a period of embryonic development during which the zygote is divided into a number of cleavage cells or *blastomeres*. Cleavage terminates with the formation of a *blastula*, which continues its development by special morphogenetic movements called *gastrulation*. The form of the blastula is a direct outgrowth of zygote structure and the pattern of cell divisions occurring during cleavage.

Cleavage divisions follow a definite pattern, characteristic of the organism. They are associated with the form of the zygote and the distribution of yolk material in it. Three basic types of ova may be recognized, *isolecithal*, *telolecithal*, and *centrolecithal*. Isolecithal ova have little yolk, about equally distributed through the cytoplasm. In telolecithal ova, the yolk is concentrated at the vegetal pole. Ova may be moderately or strongly telolecithal, depending on the quantity of yolk present. The yolk of centrolecithal ova forms a central mass.

Isolecithal ova usually cleave in a characteristic manner. The first cleavage follows the primary axis of the ovum, passing from animal to vegetal pole, producing a two-celled embryo. The whole ovum divides, so cleavage is said to be *total*, or *holoblastic*. The second division is at right angles to the first, and also passes from the animal to the vegetal poles, producing a four-celled embryo. The third cleavage is at right angles to the first two, so cutting across the primary axis. This is a transverse cleavage, and produces in embryo consisting of a quartet of blastomeres in the animal half, and a similar quartet in the vegetal half. If the two quartets are approximately equal in size, cleavage is said to be *equal*; if they are markedly dissimilar in size, it is termed *unequal*. Moderately telolecithal ova usually develop like isolecithal ova, undergoing holoblastic cleavage. However, most isolecithal ova undergo equal cleavage, while telolecithal ova usually undergo unequal clevage. The difference in size of the two quartets of cells. increases with increasing yolk. concentration at the vegetal pole.

Whether clevage is equal or unequal. the third cleavage spindles may parallel the primary axis or be at an angle to it. If the spindle parellel the main axis, the upper quartet of cells lies directly above the lower ones and clevage is *radial*. If the spindles are slanted, the cells of the upper quartet lie over the furrows between the cells of the lower quartet and clevage is said to be *spiral*. A clockwise rotation of the upper quartet of cells is caused by *dextrotropic cleavage*; a counterclockwise rotation by *levotrophic cleavage*. Generally, the members of a phylum have a characteristic type of cleavage, so this trait is useful in tracing relationships.

The cytoplasm of strongly telolecithal ova is concentrated in a small area at the aniimal pole. Only the cytoplasm divides; the large mass of yolk remains undivided. Such clevage is termed *partial* or *meroblastic*.

Centrolecithal ova have cytoplasm concentrated at the periphery of the ovum and generally the only part of the ovum to divide is the peripheral layer. Clevage of this type is *superficial*.

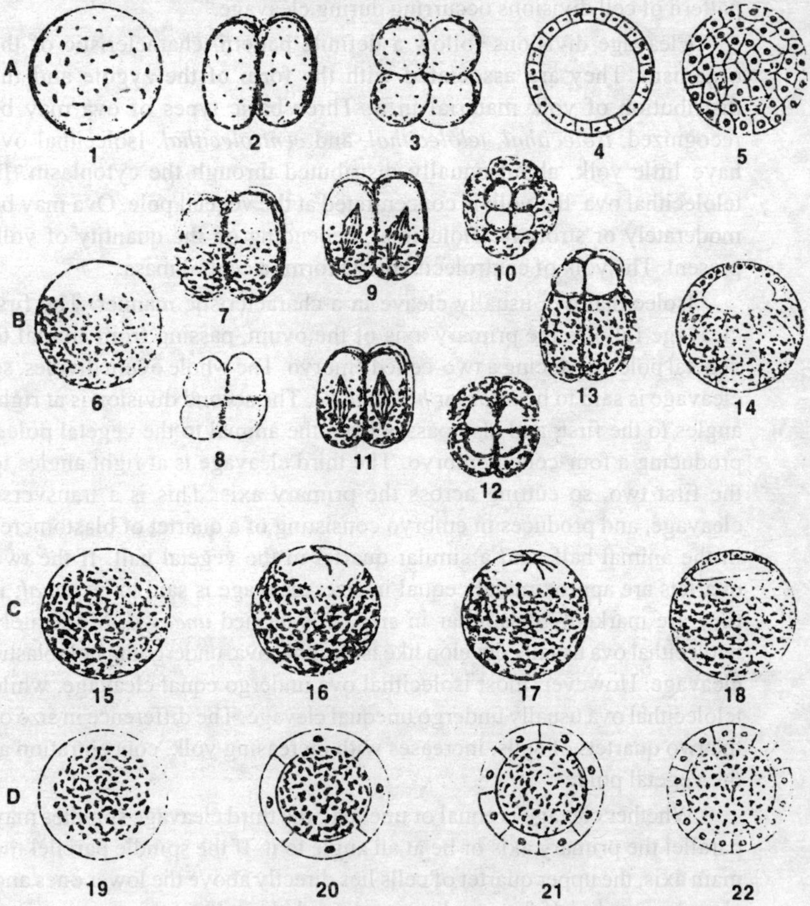

Fig. 12.1. A—(1) an isolecithal ovum, (2) Holoblastic cleavage (3) 2nd cleavage (3) Third cleavage (4)coeloblastula (5)stereoblastula. B—(6) a moderately telolecithal ovum (7) and (8) undergoing unequal holoblastic cleavage (9) & (10) undergoing spiral cleavage (11-13) radial cleavage (14) a coeloblastula. C—(15) a megalecithal egg (16 and 17) meroblastic cleavage (18) Discoblastula (19, 20, 21) superficial cleavage (22) solid blastula or periblastula.

In echinoderms, chordates, and some other kinds of animals, cleavage is *indeterminate*. When cleavage is indeterminate, the blastomeres are equally potent and the ovum has sufficient plasticity to regulate its development when injured. If the first two or four blastomeres are separated, each continues its cleavage to form a *diminutive blastula*, which in some cases continues its development to form diminutive larvae. Twins, triplets, or quadruplets can be obtained from a single zygote. In many phyla cleavage is *determinate,* and the exact destiny of the early blastomeres is determined when they are formed. When a two-celled embryo is separated into isolated cells, each produces only half of a larva. Indeterminate and determinate cleavage is also useful in recognizing relationships between phyla.

BLASTULA

The blastula varies considerably in different kinds of animals, Many blastulae have a blastocoel, located centrally if the ovum was isolecithal or displaced toward the animal pole if the ovum was telolecithal. Such hollow blastulae are called *coeloblastulae.* Others are solid, without a blastocoel, and are termed *stereoblastulae.* Stereoblastulae arise from both isolecithal and moderately telolecithal ova. Where cleavage is meroblastic, only the upper part of the zygote is divided, so that the blastula consists of a disc of cells lying on top of and undivided yolk mass. The blastocoel is reduced to the separation of cells from the yolk mass. These are known as *discoblastulae.* Centrolecithal ova, undergoing superficial cleavage, produce *periblastulae*, consisting of a continuous layer of cells surrounding a central, undivided yolk mass.

GASTRULATION–THE BEGINNING OF GERM-LAYER FORMATION

Until the blastula is fully formed, embryonic development is dominated by cleavage divisions. The blastula is transformed into a gastrula by cell movements known as *gastrulation*. Gastrulation is accomplished in a variety of ways, but in all cases starts the formation of the germ layers. The most important methods are *invagination, epiboly, involution, delamination,* and *ingression.*

Gastrulation by invagination occurs in many coeloblastulae and is the type most commonly emphasized in introductory texts. The vegetal hemisphere of the blastula pushes inward to form a saccate space, the *gastrocoel*, also known as the *archenteron* and the *primitive gut*. The gastrocoel opens to the exterior through the *blastopore.* As invagination proceeds, the gastrocoel grows at the expense of the blastocoel. The blastocoel may be completely obliterated or may persist as a fairly large cavity. Although fairly important as a method of gastrulation, it is less common than some of the other methods.

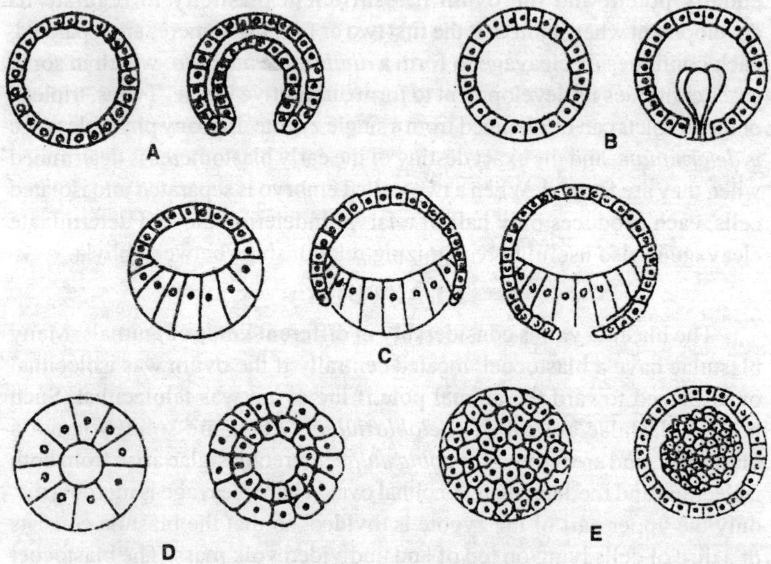

Fig. 12.2. Types of Blastulae and Methods of Gastrulation. A—A coeloblastula with a central blastocoel, undergoing gastrulation by invagination. B—A similar blastula undergoing gastrulation by polar ingression. In this case, no blastopore is formed. C—A coeloblastula with the blastocoel displaced toward the animal pole, undergoing gastrulation by epiboly. D—A blastula with large cells undergoing gastrulation by tangential cell division. E—A stereoblastula gastrulating by delamination.

Gastrulation by epiboly and involution are probably modifications of gastrulation by invagination. They occur in animals with telolecithal ova, where the large amount of yolk in the vegetal hemisphere makes invagination of blastomeres difficult or impossible. Where unequal cleavage has produced large macromeres at the vegetal pole and micromeres at the animal pole, the smaller, more active cells may move down over the larger, more inert, yolk-filled cells. This movement is epiboly. It results in a gastrula with a blastopore at the vegetal pole and with at least a vestige of a gastrocoel. Gastrulation by involution is most commonly seen in discoblastulae produced by meroblastic cleavage. At some point, usually related to the future symmetry of the organism, cells turn inward and move back under the surface cells and over the yolk mass. This produces a doubled surface layer separated from the yolk by a small space, the rudiment of the gastrocoel. Evidently this type of gastrula is highly modified and lacks a typical blastopore or gastrocoel. As it develops from a discoblastula, it is called a *discogastrula*.

Gastrulation by invagination, epiboly, or involution produces a gastrula with a central cavity or some vestige of it, usually opening to the outside by a blastopore. This type of gastrula is called a *coelogastrula.*

When gastrulation occurs by delamination or ingression, however, there is nothing comparable to a blastopore and there may be no evidence of a gastrocoel. This type of gastrula is a *stereogastrula.* Gastrulation by delamination may occur in either of two ways. A coeloblastula may produce a two layered gastrula by tangential cell divisions, cutting off the inner portions of the blastomeres as an inner mass of cells. This obscures the central cavity, or produces a gastrula without an opening to the interior cavity. Stereoblastulae can gastrulate by delamination through the separation of the outer cells from an inner cell mass. This usually involves a sorting out process, accompanied by flattening of the outer cells; it produces a solid gastrula without gastrocoel or blastopore. Gastrulation by ingression occurs when surface cells migrate to the interior. Ingression may be unipolar, occurring only at one pole, or multipolar, occurring at various points on the blastula surface. Ingression forms a gastrula without gastrocoel or blastopore. Unipolar ingression may be a modification of invagination.

Gastrulation produces a two-layered embryo, composed of the primary germ layers. The outer layer is the ectoderm and the inner layer the endoderm. If present, the gastrocoel is the primordium of the digestive cavity, and the blastopore may be thought of as the primitive, embryonic mouth. For reasons that will become evident later, the gastrula is of considerable interest in speculation about evolutionary relationships. The blastopore is sometimes retained as the adult mouth; sometimes it is closed off and a secondary mouth is formed some distance away. Same divide the animal kingdom into two main branches, the *Protostomata,* which retain the blastopore as a mouth, and the *Deuterostomata,* which form a new mouth some distance away from the closed blastopore.

MESODERM-THE THIRD GERM LAYER

Despite dissimilarities in the form of gastrulae and in the methods of gastrulation, gastrulae have some remarkably constant features. That a two layered embryo should have inner and outer layers is scarcely surprising, but it is remarkable that these layers should tend to form the same body parts, even in dissimilar animals with dissimilar gastrulae arising by diverse methods of gastrulation. The ectoderm of most animals gives rise to the outer, epithelial covering of the body and its derivatives, to the lining of the most anterior and posterior parts of the digestive tract, and to the nervous system and sense organs. The endoderm gives rise to the epithelial lining of the remainder of the digestive tract, and the glands and other derivatives arising from it. Since all of the cells of a typical gastrula are a part of either the inner or outer layers, it is evident that all other tissues must also arise from them. However, this is brought about by forming a third germ layer, the *mesoderm.* Mesoderm forms in a variety of ways and at varied times during development. As it is derived from endoderm or ectoderm, it is considered a secondary germ layer, while the other layers are the primary germ layers. Ectoderm and endoderm are more or less homologous throughout the animal kingdom, except, possibly, in the sponges. Mesoderm, on the other hand, is more variable. There is evidence of two kinds of mesoderm, which may or may not be considered similar enough to be homologous.

Mesoderm arises either as a loose connective tissue or as an epithelial layer. The loose type of mesoderm is called *mesenchyme.* Mesoderm is mesenchymal in sponges, coelenterates, and ctenophores. In these phyla, all of the mesoderm is derived from the ectoderm and so may be called *ectomesoderm.* In all other metazoans, the bulk of the mesoderm arises from the endoderm and is called *endomesoderm*. While ectomesoderm is invariably mesenchymal, endomesoderm may be epithelial or mesenchymal. It arises at such different times and in such varied ways that it is doubtful that all endomesoderm can be considered homologous. Nevertheless, extensive correlation of the endomesodermal derivatives among diverse animals gives support to the germ-layer concept.

Ectomesoderm arises by simple ingression of cells from the ectoderm. The space between the ectoderm and endoderm is occupied by a jelly-like matirx, the *mesogloea,* which comes to have a greater or lesser population of cells depending on the extent of cellular ingression. This type of mesoderm formation was not recognized at first, and the phyla with ectomesoderm were once called diploblastic, or two-layered.

Endomesoderm formation is too diverse to discuss in detail here. In some animals, all of the mesoderm arises from a special blastomere, formed during early cleavage. In others it arises as a mesenchymal mass, and in still other it appears as an epithelial tissue stemming from the endoderm.

BODY CAVITIES (COELOM)

Metazoan architecture is best understood by considering the relationship of the germ layers and their derivatives to the important body cavities. The blastocoel is the first cavity to appear and parts of it may persist in adults. The gastrocoel is generally permanent, forming the digestive cavity. Sponges are exceptional, in that the system of cavities is entirely unlike those found in other animals, indicating an independent line of descent. In the most primitive Eumetazoa, the gastrocoel is the only embryonic cavity and the digestive cavity is the only body cavity of the adult. This is true of the Cnidaria and Ctenophora and of the acoelomate Bilateria.

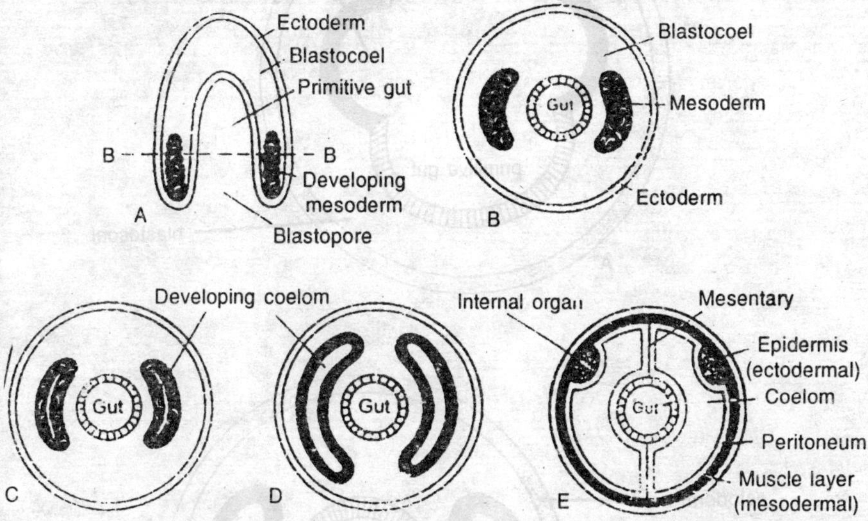

Fig. 12.3. Origin of the coelom by schizocoely. A—Frontal section of a late gastrula, B—Cross section of gastrula at level indicated in A, C—Coelom developing as a split (schizocoel) in the mesodermal mass, D—Further development of the mesoderm and coelom. Note that the old blastocoel is gradually obliterated, E—Cross section through an adult coelomate protostome. Muscle layer develops from mesoderm. Internal organs lie behind peritoneum (retroperitoneal) which lines coelom.

In Aschelminthes and higher invertebrates, the mesoderm does not completely fill the space between the digestive tube and body wall. A *body cavity* is present, separating the body wall from the digestive tube. There are two kinds of body cavities, the *pseudocoelom* and *coelom*. In animals with a pseudocoelom, the mesoderm adjacent to the digestive tube is mesenchymal, and eventually disappears as the spongy spaces unite to form a large space. In these animals the body wall is lined with mesodermal tissue, but separated from the digestive tube by the pseudocoelom. In animals with a true coelom, the coelomic space appears within the mesoderm. As a result, the body wall is lined with mesoderm and the digestive tract is covered by it.

A true coelom may be formed in either of two ways. If the mesoderm arises as mesenchyme, it is at first a solid mass filling the space between

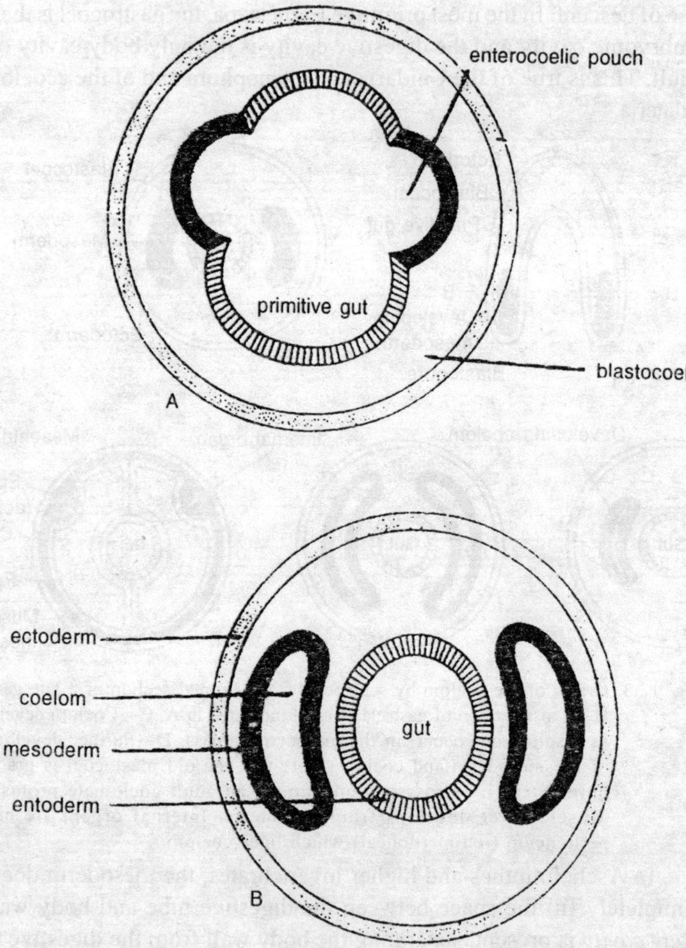

Fig. 12.4. Mesoderm and coelom formation by enterocoelic pouching. A—lateral evaginations of wall or primitive gut. B—Separation of pouches to form coelom, mesoderm, and definitive gut entoderm.

ectoderm and endoderm. Delamination occurs, resulting in the separation of an outer somatic layer and an inner splanchnic layer. The somatic layer adheres to the body wall and the splanchnic layer to the digestive tube. The coelomic space is thus completely surrounded by mesodermal tissue. When the coelom develops in this way, development is *schizocoelous*. Where the mesoderm arises as a pouch or double epithelial layer arising, from the endoderm, somatic and splanchnic layers are foreshadowed from the start, and the coelom is, in a sense, a derivative of the digestive cavity. This type of development is termed *enterocoelous*.

ORIGIN OF METAZOA

Metazoa constitute all the multicellular organisms. It includes sponges, coelenterates, helminths, worms, arthropods, molluscs, echinoderms and chordates. All the zoologists agree that metazoans evolved from unicellular organisms, but opinions differ as to the particular group of unicellular forms involved and the mode of origin. There is also disagreement about the mode of origin. The current theories can be grouped around three principal viewpoints that :

1. The metazoan arose from a multinucleate ciliate that became cellularized.
2. The ancestral metazoan arose by way of a colonial flagellate through cellular specialization and interdependence.
3. The metazoans have had a polyphylatic origin from different unicellular groups of protozoans.

Theories for the origin of metazoa

There are three main theories to explain the origin of metazoans. They are as follows:

1. Syncytial Theory
2. Colonial Theory
3. Polyphylatic Theory

1. Syncytial Theory

This theory was proposed by *Hadzi* (1953) and *Henson* (1977). According to this theory the metazoans arose from a primitive group of multinucleate ciliates. This single called multinucleate resembled the present day *Opalina*. The ancestral metazoan was at first syncytial but later on acquired cell membranes and changed into a compartmented form, thus producing a multicellular structure. Because many ciliates tend towards bilateral symmetry, proponents of the syncytial theory hold the view that (a) the ancestral metazoan was bilaterally symmetrical and (b) gave rise to acoel flat worms, which are regarded to be most primitive living metazoans.

The fact that the acoels are in the same size range as the ciliates, are bilaterally symmetrical and tend towards a syncytial condition is considered as evidence supporting the primitive position of this group. Further, the ciliate macronucleus, which is absent in acoels, is supposed to have been absent in the multinucleate prociliate stock from which the metazoan arose.

The macronucleus is assumed to have developed later in evolutionary line leading to higher ciliates.

Objections

There are a number of objections to this theory. Nothing comparable to cellularization occurs in the ontogeny of any these groups. Although cellularization does occur in the superficial cleavage of arthropod eggs, but this is a highly specilalized condition associated with a large amount of yolk. As a matter of fact, the syncytial nature of acoel tissue arises secondarily after typical, cytosomal, embryonic divisions. Moreover, a ciliate ancestory does not explain the general occurrence of a flagellated sperm in metazoans. No such cells are produced in ciliates and it is necessary to assume a *de noro* origin of motile sperm in ancestral metazoan. The most serious objection to the syncytial theory is that if we accept this theory we must also accept that the acoels are the most primitive living metazoans. Bilateral symmetry then becomes the primitive symmetry for metazoans, and the radially symmetrical coelenterates must be derived secondarily from the flatworms.

2. Colonial Theory

This theory was proposed by *Haeckel* (1874), later modified by *Metschnikoff* (1887) and revived by *Hyman* (1940). This theory maintains that the flagellates are ancestors of the matazoans. *Haeckel* believed that the first metazoan originated from a *Volvox* like colony. He proposed a theory for the origin of metazoa. This theory is called *gastraea theory*. According to him the metazoan was originated from a hypothetical ancestor called *blastea*. The blastea rsembles the existing *Volvox*. In all multicellular animals the blastea stage is represented by the *blastula* stage of development. The blastea is a spherical and hollow. It has a single layer of flagellated cells.

The first metazoan was originated from the blastea by the invagination of te cells present in the posterior region. This invagination produced a primitive double-walled organism, the *gastraea*. The gastraea had two layers, outer ectoderm and inner endoderm. The endoderm encloses the cavity which functions as a gut and its opening as mouth. The gastraea is equivalent to the gastrula stage which is formed in the embryonic development. In addition to embryological evidence, *Haeckel* also noted the close similarity in structure between gastraea and some lower metazoans such as sponges and hydrozoan cnidarian both of which are doubled-walled with a single opening, the mouth (paragastric cavity in sponges and gastro-vascular cavity in hydrozoan cnidarians—rather in all coelenterates).

Metschnikoff later on modified the Haeckel's gastraea. He noted that the primitive mode of gastrulation in coelenterates is by *ingression*, in which the cells are proliferated from the blastula wall into the interior blastocoel so that the blastula is changed with a solid gastrula, *stereogastrula*. The inner mass of cells represents endoderm and outer layer represents the ectoderm. According to *Metschnikoff*, contrary to the contention of *Haeckel* about gastrula formation by invagination, the invagination is apparently a secondary embryonic short cut, the primitive mode of gastrulation is by ingression. Contrary to the contention of *Haeckel*, *Metschnikoff*, therefore, argued that the gastraea was a solid rather than a hollow organism in the ancestory of metazoans.

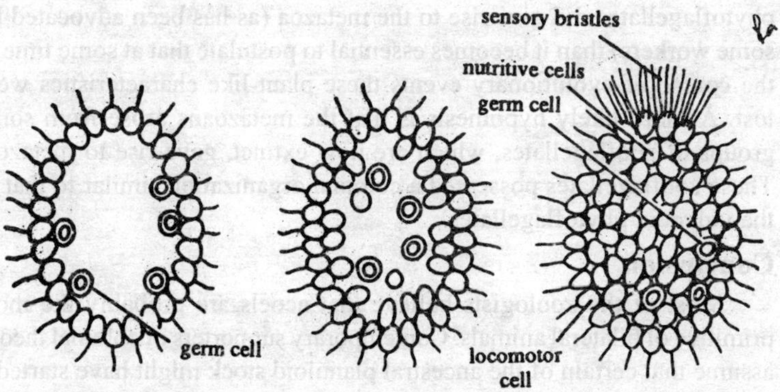

Fig. 12.5. A—Hypothetical ancestral blasta , B—Multipolar ingression, C—Hypothetical planuloid antestor.

In accordance with Metchnikoff's revision, modern elaborators of the Colonial Theory pick up the evolution of the metazoans with the Haeckel's blastaea. Through the inward proliferation of the cells originally hollow sphere changed into an organism having a solid structure. The body of this hypothetical ancestor is believed to have been ovoid and radially symmetrical. The outer cells were flagellated and performed a locomotor sensory function. The solid mass of interior cells functioned in nutrition and reproduction. There was no mouth so food could be engulfed anywhere on the outer surface and passed to the interior. As this hypothetical organism closely resembles the planula larva of coelenterates, it has been called the *planuloid ancestor*.

From such a free-swimming planuloid ancestor the lower metazoans are believed to have arisen. On the basis of this theory, the primary radial symmetry of the coelenterates can be said to be derived directly from the planuloid ancestor. The bilateral symmetry of the acoelomate flat worms would have represent a later modification in symmetry.

3. Prophylatic Theory

This theory was proposed by *Greenberg* (1959). This theory proposes that two different types of ancestors for metazoans. One ancestor is colonial flagellate which gave rise to sponges and coelenterates and second ancestor is a ciliate which gave rise to ctenophore and flatworms.

The existing flagellates that fulfill the qualification for metazoan ancestors are the fresh water phytoflagellate *Volvox*. These plant like organisms have cellulose cell-walls, chlorophyll, autotrophic nutrition and go through the reduction divisions following fertilization. If the phytoflagellates did give rise to the metazoa (as has been advocated by some workers) than it becomes essential to postulate that at some time in the course of evolutionary events these plant-like characteristics were lost. A more likely hypothesis is that the metazoans arose from some groups of zooflagellates, which are now extinct, gave rise to metazoa. These zooflagellates possessed a colonial organization similar to that in the volvocid phytoflagellates.

Conclusion

Most of the zoologists believe that acoels are probably the most primitive of bilateral animals. Contemporary supporters of colonial theory assume that certain of the ancestral planuloid stock might have started a life on the ocean floor and as a result developed a creeping mode of locomotion over rocks and other such objects. This could have led to a differentiation between dorsal and ventral surfaces and to the development of mouth on ventral side. Such differentiation would have produced a bilateral symmetry and would have led to the evolution of primitive flatworms.

PLACOZOA

Trichoplax adharens is a minute animal-like, multicellular organism discovered in a European sea-water aquarium in 1883 and has since been cultured and studied many times. Its body is flat, the lower surface is concave and upper flat. The body is composed of two layers of flagellated epitheloid cells, which lodge between them an inner layer of loose, contractile, stellate cells-like mesenchyma. The margin of the body is irregular. The animal changes shape like an amoeba. It creeps over the substratum by means of its flagella and feeds upon minute organic particles. The organic particles are engulfed by the cells of the lower epithelium. The organism undergoes asexual reproduction by fission and by budding.

However, eggs arising from the ventral epithelium have been also observed within the internal mesenchyme-like layer. The DNA content is smaller than that found in any other animal.

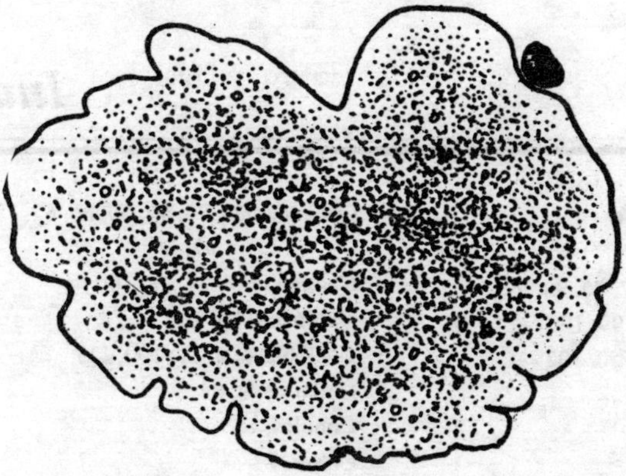

Fig. 12.6. *Trichoplax adherens* (Dorsal view)

In the beginning the zoologists regarded that *Trichoplax* was a larval stage of some unidentified animal. However, now it has become established without any doubt that it is indeed an adult organism and not a larva. *Trichoplax* may represent the most primitive living metazoan because it possesses a number of features speculated for the planuloid ancestor described above and it is for this reason that after dealing with various view on Metazoan origin in the above paragraphs the account of *Trichoplax* has been given here at the end.

Revision Questions

1. Write an essay on the Origin of Metazoa.
2. Give an account of Hadzi's theory regarding Origin of Metazoa.
3. Describe the colonial theory of Origin of Metazoa.

Index